YOU ARE NOT ALONE

This book brings together the key events in the lives of 14 ethnically diverse school leaders and members of the NAHT 'Leaders for Race Equality' group through school, university, interviews and promotion. The group was established in 2020 in response to the events of the pandemic and the murder of George Floyd, providing support to its members leading schools through this challenging time.

The featured school leaders provide their own personal accounts of the barriers and challenges they faced during their own education and into their roles as school leaders, including how they overcame adversity to achieve their goals. Common to many stories is the impact of the school environment and how vital the support and influence of role models can be, and the book concludes by setting out key recommendations for schools and policy makers. Including forewords from two prominent black contributors in the field, this important text aims to change attitudes, build allies and inspire other individuals to aim for their goals and know that you are not alone.

This book will be of benefit to all school leaders at both primary and secondary levels. It will be an important read for those looking to support colleagues and understand the need for diversity and equity among teaching and leadership staff.

NAHT is the definitive voice of school leaders, working to create a better education system for both educationalists and students alike. They represent over 38,000 school leaders, making it the largest association for school leaders in the United Kingdom. The 'Leaders for Race Equality' group provides a space for members to come together to discuss the experiences and issues facing them as school leaders within NAHT and the profession more widely.

YOU ARE NOT ALONE

14 STORIES FROM EDUCATION

BY LEADERS FOR RACE EQUALITY

Edited by NAHT

LONDON AND NEW YORK

First published 2025
by Routledge
4 Park Square, Milton Park, Abingdon, Oxon OX14 4RN

and by Routledge
605 Third Avenue, New York, NY 10158

Routledge is an imprint of the Taylor & Francis Group, an informa business

© 2025 selection and editorial matter, NAHT; individual chapters, the contributors

The right of NAHT to be identified as the author of the editorial material, and of the authors for their individual chapters, has been asserted in accordance with sections 77 and 78 of the Copyright, Designs and Patents Act 1988.

All rights reserved. No part of this book may be reprinted or reproduced or utilised in any form or by any electronic, mechanical, or other means, now known or hereafter invented, including photocopying and recording, or in any information storage or retrieval system, without permission in writing from the publishers.

Trademark notice: Product or corporate names may be trademarks or registered trademarks, and are used only for identification and explanation without intent to infringe.

British Library Cataloguing-in-Publication Data
A catalogue record for this book is available from the British Library

ISBN: 978-1-032-80559-7 (hbk)
ISBN: 978-1-032-81201-4 (pbk)
ISBN: 978-1-003-49861-2 (ebk)

DOI: 10.4324/9781003498612

Typeset in Palatino
by SPi Technologies India Pvt Ltd (Straive)

In memory of
Yvonne Conolly, Britain's first female black Head Teacher

Contents

Acknowledgments ix
Foreword by Diana Osagie x
Foreword by Paul Miller xii
Disclaimer xvii

Introduction 1
LORNA LEGG

1 I'm not Aunty, I'm your teacher 4
AMA OSAPANIN

2 Changing the narrative: How I transformed labels into opportunities for growth and forged my own path 10
DANIELLE LEWIS-EGONU

3 My leadership journey 16
DEBBIE DOHERTY

4 Best fit 22
DIANA OHENE-DARKO

5 Challenging times 27
ELAINE WILLIAMS

6 It takes a village to raise a child 32
LORNA LEGG

7 All I ever wanted to be was a teacher 38
MAYLEEN ATIMA

Contents

8	Coming out BAME: two moments RICK STUART-SHEPPARD	43
9	Your career is a marathon, not a sprint ROSS ASHCROFT	49
10	An epiphany RUHAINA ALFORD-RAHIM	57
11	Learning, growing and finding your light SABRINA EDWARDS	62
12	Children can't be what they can't see: Breaking the cycle SARAH HOBSON	69
13	Overcoming stereotypes: Embracing your value on the path to leadership SYMONE CAMPBELL	75
14	Focused, determined and resilient YVONNE DAVIS	81
15	Culture and ethos: Additional chapter DIANA OHENE-DARKO	88
16	Curriculum change: Additional chapter DANIELLE LEWIS-EGONU	94
17	Recruitment and retention of a diverse workforce: Additional chapter LORNA LEGG	98

Acknowledgments

We would like to offer thanks to:

Lorna Legg, who had the idea for this book and worked with other members of Leaders for Race Equality to bring their stories together; Paul Whiteman, General Secretary of NAHT, who generously said, 'Yes!' to the original book, and to Natalie Pettifer, Leaders for Race Equality group coordinator, who supported this group and the book from the start and took the initial idea seriously; the Leaders for Race Equality group, who have opened up so many possibilities, simply by sharing and supporting each other; Debbie Doherty and Ross Ashcroft, group members, who put aside time to read submissions with us; Diana Osagie and Professor Paul Miller, who have been kind enough to write such thoughtful and hopeful forewords; all those working towards equality, diversity and inclusion and all those who have simply been our role models.

Foreword by Diana Osagie

Diana Osagie, Founder of Courageous Leadership & The Academy of Women's Leadership

I love a challenge. Leadership of a school in the urban landscape of north London for many years was both the biggest nightmare and greatest pleasure of my professional career. I have gone on to set up two businesses that create courageous leaders, teach an MA in Educational Leadership and give keynote addresses across the nation. Regularly I am asked the question, 'How did you rise to the top of leadership as a black woman?' I want the answer to be,

I didn't rise as a black woman!

I rose as a talented leader

I rose as a skilled practitioner

I rose because I was the best person for the role

However; race, gender, the way you look, the way you speak, the lifestyle your parents could afford, all have a voice in the interview room. Silently speaking a narrative that you ignore at your peril.

My voice is loud, my voice is articulate and my voice is experienced. But for some on the other side of the table looking at me as I answer their questions, *they are hearing the voice of skin colour*. It's a voice in their head, pregnant with bias and stereotype. Is it possible to amplify the words from my mouth and silence the perceived voice of my skin?

This book is an important read. It is not your typical leadership book. The voice of young black and Asian leaders is here.

Foreword by Diana Osagie

Talented, skilled and ambitious, the leaders in this book tell their stories of how their skin speaks louder than their mouths in certain situations as they navigate the leadership landscape.

Some of these stories will elicit sadness. Some will make you question why? How is that possible? Why do people treat others that way? Whatever emotion rises when you read, don't stop reading! Keep engaging with the narrative these leaders present to you and imagine yourself or your child facing these obstacles as they try to establish themselves in society.

As I read the following from one author, it forced me to reflect on what is a reality for many global majority leaders.

Have you ever wondered if you fit the bill? Are you the right (acceptable) colour? Do you speak (acceptably) well? I'm a light shade of brown, olive skin some might say. I speak well, pronouncing my 't's and 'f's correctly. I'm an acceptable shade it would seem. But I know colleagues who have not been afforded the same recognition. Nothing is ever said of course but 'best fit' often wins the day after interview.

Storytelling is a pillar of society. We hand down the narrative of our lives to the next generation with the hope that they do not repeat our mistakes and they remember to celebrate the past victories. Reading this book gives you a stake in the changing of the narrative of racism and bias, which has hurt our society and made us all morally poorer. We all now have the opportunity to read, understand and change.

Diversity of people around the leadership table is a strength and an asset to any organisation. It adds a wealth of experience, a variety of lenses on the world and a balance of perspective that serves our schools well.

As one author said, 'We are a flavoursome array of heritages, beliefs and traditions. And I wouldn't have it any other way'.

Foreword by Paul Miller

Paul Miller PhD, Professor of Educational Leadership & Social Justice

I am pleased to write the foreword to this timely book. In my view, this book is important for two main reasons, first, there is not a lot of available written material, written by school leaders, about their experiences and practice, and second, there is no previously available compilation of 'reflective case studies' written entirely by school leaders, let alone, school leaders of BAME heritage. This is indeed a watershed moment!

As I mentioned in my 2018 book, *The Nature of School Leadership: Global Practice Perspectives*, 'Until very recently, much of literature and research on school leadership did not give primacy to the voice of school leaders. That is, although school leaders were the subject of intense research, they were often spoken for in published accounts of their working and/or working lives' (Miller, 2018, p. 11). According to Hughes (1976), the relative absence of the voice of school leaders in presenting their own stories has meant their lived realities and experiences are not always prioritised in the educational leadership literature and research. This absence of the leaders' voice in presenting their own stories has resulted in 'a general failure to come to grips with the "street realities" of headship' (Ball 1994, p. 8). Wolcott (1973), in 'The Man in the Principal's Office' noted there is much to be gained from capturing the accounts of what school leaders do and what they experience during the course of their duties versus what is felt they experience or what is felt school leaders should do. Bolman & Heller (1995) argue that much of the literature on leadership is irrelevant to school leaders as it is 'too abstract and detached from practice or too narrow and disengaged from person and context, and therefore, of little use to those in schools' (p. 342).

The 14 reflective case studies provided in this book are not presented as 'empirical research', but rather as reflective accounts of their educational and leadership journeys in England. They are important as they are unique since, each is written from 'a particular place and time, [and] from a history and a culture, which is specific' (Blackmore, 2009, p. 222). Presented in the form of an integrated analysis, each case study broadens, and simultaneously deepens our understanding of the unique educational experiences encountered by each school leader enroute to a leadership role. Furthermore, each case study offers 'descriptions of leaders in action ... and detailed descriptions of them at work' (Southworth, 1993, p. 79), highlighting the 'little stuff of everyday life' (Blasé & Anderson, 1995, p. 25), the 'the nitty gritty' (Miller, 2016, p. 1) of their humanity, and the 'street realities' (Ball, 1994, p. 8) of a school leader of BAME heritage in England in 2020.

The reflective case studies disrupt the taken for granted assumptions that 'equates [leadership] with being white (in Western countries), male, heterosexual, middle class and middle aged' (Coleman, 2012, p. 597). Equally the case stories bespeak stories of hurt, of degradation, of hope, of courage, of triumph. For the first time in the field of educational leadership we see a book written entirely by school leaders; and for the first time in the field of educational leadership, we see a book written exclusively by school leaders of BAME heritage. The authors therefore own their story, the story of BAME school leadership in England; and they narrate their own stories, not relying on these to be told by someone else, nor risking these be misrepresented. These case stories are uniquely cathartic, providing glimpses of who they are as individuals and as leaders, of how far they have come, and of their imagined future for themselves, their families, and for all who study and work in the schools they lead. Theirs is therefore a story of sub-verting structural and institutional racism, of resilience, of identity, and of belonging. As provided by Stuart-Sheppard, 'My journey to wholeness or completeness or acceptance of my identity has been lifelong and the moment of revelation was unexpected', and by Alford-Rahim, 'The desire to be the same is quite a powerful urge when you doubt your place in society or fear rejection because of your difference'.

Foreword by Paul Miller

Crucially, these case studies mean that teachers and students of BAME heritage in England now have a 'reference book of hope and inspiration' from role models they identify with ethnically and culturally, breaking with deeply embedded and stereotypical notions of who [should] aspire and inhabit leadership roles. For example, Edwards noted she wanted, 'To be that inspirational teacher that switches something on in a child; helps them to see who they are; where they've come from and who they could become', underlining Ashcroft's asserting of his 'dual-heritage, mixed-raced, non-white, mixed Black Caribbean and White British' identity. For Atima, it was equally simple, 'All I ever wanted to be was a teacher and I have achieved that goal'.

This book then has consequences for those who currently study and work in our schools, and for those who ultimately aspire to and attain school leadership roles. As provided by Anon, 'I want to be part of the next generation of leaders; leaders who have equality on the agenda; leaders who 'see' everyone and are bold enough to make changes. I want to be that change. I want to make a difference. I want to leave a small part of the world better than I found it.' The book also has consequences for those leading and governing our schools. As provided by Campbell, 'It is imperative to have diverse leaders and governors in school leadership running our schools to improve the awareness of different races, cultures, religion and economic status, ensuring they understand and can identify with the experiences of their whole school community and more importantly, having open and honest discussions'. This view was echoed by Legg who called for, 'Mandatory, national training for all governors and staff, preferably also parents and pupils, in implicit bias, would be a good place to start redressing any disadvantage and open up leadership to a more representative and diverse group of people'.

Racism and race discrimination can and does undermine those who experience it. This can sometimes lead people of BAME heritage to conflate everyday 'bad' experiences as racist experiences. This is noted by Doherty who provides, 'Racism is systemic, but if you are unsuccessful in securing a leadership role, don't immediately assume that it's because of

Foreword by Paul Miller

implicit, explicit racial discrimination although, as we are acutely aware, that may well be the case'. The emergence of a more 'sophisticated racism' makes Doherty's point both poignant and problematic, challenging society and those in the teaching profession to be alert to acts of micro-aggression and micro-incivilities and how these could lead to a narrow pool of applicants or people putting themselves forward due to fatigue or stress or both. Lewis-Egonu acknowledges this conundrum by arguing, 'Experiencing discrimination can provoke stress responses similar to post-traumatic stress disorder and therefore BAME staff need to feel supported by leadership in their school. The negative treatment affects an individual's life and wellbeing'. Despite the effects of racism, there is hope. Davis recounts the words of her mom, 'that's why you need to be there', and Hobson-Riley, 'My focus is the children I work with and providing them with a quality education, but I also realise that I am changing children's mindsets, as they are also learning that leaders can also look like me'. Furthermore, Osapanin clarifies, 'I know that, and have the confidence these days, to confront those situations. But as an NQT, I didn't have that confidence. For years as a class teacher I didn't either'.

As a whole, this book presents a strong counter-narrative to the victim narrative of racism. After qualifying as a teacher, Williams found getting a job much harder than she'd imagined. She reflected, 'I felt that I had been lied to. Why let me spend time completing a teaching degree if I'd never be good enough to secure a job? Why grade me so highly on assignments and school experiences if I'd never get a chance to have my own class?' Later however she would recall, 'there I was, Head Teacher of a small rural primary school. I was the only black person there; no other black staff, no black children'.

The case studies in this book confirms that the journey to headship is a fraught one, more so for teachers of BAME heritage than white staff. Nevertheless, these case studies also offer every student and teacher of BAME heritage hope and inspiration that success against, and despite, the tide is possible.

REFERENCES

Ball, S. J. (1994). *Education Reform: A Critical and Post Structural Approach*. Buckingham: Open University Press.

Blackmore, J. (2009). International Response Essay, Leadership for Social Justice: A Transnational Dialogue. *Journal of Research on Leadership Education*, 4(1): 1–10.

Blasé, J., & Anderson, G. (1995). *The Micropolitics of Educational Leadership: From Control to Empowerment*. London: Cassell.

Bolman, L. G., & Heller, R. (1995). Research on School Leadership: The State-of-the-Art. In S. B. Bacharach & B. Mundell (Eds.), *Images of Schools: Structures and Roles in Organizational Behavior*. Thousand Oaks, CA: Corwin Press Inc.

Coleman, M. (2012). Leadership and Diversity, *Educational Leadership and Management*, 40(5): 592–609.

Hughes, M. (1976). The Professional-as-Administrator: The Case of the Secondary School Head. In R. S. Peters (Ed.), *The Role of the Head*. London: Routledge & Kegan Paul.

Miller, P. (2016). *Exploring School Leadership in England and the Caribbean: New Insights from a Comparative Approach*. London: Bloomsbury

Miller, P. (2018). *The Nature of School Leadership: Global Practice Perspectives*. London: Palgrave Macmillan.

Southworth, G. (1993). School Leadership and School Development: Reflections from Research. *School Organisation*, 13(1): 73–87.

Wolcott, H. (1973). *The Man in the Principal's Office: An Ethnography*. New York: Holt, Rinehart & Winston, Inc.

Disclaimer

The views and examples shared in this book are those of individuals, rather than being official NAHT policy or advice.

In sharing our stories, we have used a range of words to describe the various groups to which we belong. In doing so, we acknowledge that terms may change over time; they may gain negative connotations and fall out of use or favour. We ask that you forgive us if we cause offence. Our aim is not to offend, but to extend understanding of the experiences that have shaped us. Where we describe ourselves in terms used by others, intended to offend us, we do so to call them out and expose them. Where we describe ourselves, please accept the terms used as our chosen ones. Where we describe others, we try to use terms that treat people with respect.[1]

NOTE

1 www.sharewords.com/biasfree.html Accessed online 10.1.21.
   Basically, bias-free language means using terms that treat people with respect. Sometimes it means leaving out certain kinds of words altogether, such as not describing someone's physical characteristics when doing so serves no purpose. The three most important guidelines found and which work in every case:

   1. Whether you are describing a group of people or individuals, ask them what terminology they use.
   2. If you can't do that, be as specific as possible.
   3. Keep the person in the description: people who are blind (not the blind).

   https://apastyle.apa.org/style-grammar-guidelines/bias-free-language/racial-ethnic-minorities.

Introduction

Lorna Legg

The NAHT Leaders for Race Equality group began in response to the events of 2020; a year unlike any other. Together, we responded to the growing pandemic, leading schools through this most challenging time. We discovered that people from Black, Asian and other ethnic groups experience higher death rates from Covid-19, compared to White ethnic groups; and we saw, with horror, the murder of George Floyd on 25 May. The Black Lives Matter movement, and the sharing, online, of racist, sexist, homophobic, Islamophobic and Anti-Semitic incidents in Britain and across the world, have spurred many of us on, to educate ourselves and find new ways to end the stereotyping, stigma and structural inequality that cause so much pain and waste so much potential.

There is still much to do. Jane Elliott's seminal 'Blue Eyes/Brown Eyes' lesson, which she first gave on 5 April 1968, the day after Martin Luther King Jr. was assassinated (see 'A Class Divided') is still ground-breaking in its approach to counteracting prejudice and bias, but further work is beginning to be shared, for example, group member Sabrina Edwards' 'Educating for Equality' course has been inspirational. We also need to look beyond school, at the society which influences us. In her novel, *Girl, Woman, Other*, Bernadine Evaristo, 2019 Booker Prize winner, exemplified this beautifully:

> Classroom walls are decorated with … a map of the world that makes Britain rival Africa in size, testament to cartographers who got away with it for centuries, even now, it seems
>
> (p. 219)

But there is hope in the diverse, historic voices and faces, once side-lined, who now have a new audience; giving greater depth to our shared history and counteracting the legacy of colonialism.

Into this context, the NAHT, under the leadership of Paul Whiteman, acknowledged a lack of diversity and representation in the union. To their lasting credit, they started the process of change, setting up the (then) BAME NAHT group. In the very first meeting, facilitated by Natalie Pettifer (our advocate and Regional Organiser), members first shared their experiences of rejection and exclusion, with many of them moved to tears:

> At our meeting, we each shared our personal and challenging stories of the discrimination we have faced as leaders and listened to each other's struggles and truths. It was quite a candid and enlightening experience and it got emotional at times as I think it made us realise that we aren't alone in this.
> Leaders for Race Equality member,
> Sara Wilkinson, 25 July 2020

Elements of those stories now form the basis of this book, which distils key events in the lives of 14 leaders in education from Asian, African, Caribbean and multiple backgrounds, through school, university, interviews and promotion. A group of us wrote a summary of our experiences, and common threads emerged, which we only saw in hindsight. With the group's enthusiasm, the commitment of Natalie Pettifer and solid support of Paul Whiteman, it was possible to ask creative book designer, Michelle Abadie, to guide us. As the group began to write, members Ross Ashcroft and Deborah Doherty helped me read submissions, and many members offered suggestions, advice and support. In the spirit of true collaboration, this project was made possible.

To tell the truth about difficult situations is brave; it can feel like an even greater step beyond your comfort zone, if standing out has not always been a positive experience. Yet the people in this book have already shown their courage, in deciding to overcome incidents of ignorance and prejudice to get closer to their goal: to help children and young people achieve theirs. Common to many stories is the impact of the school environment and how vital the support and influence of role models can be.

'You cannot be what you cannot see' is an idea explored in a BBC article (28 July 2020), about Aretha Banton (Vice Principal) and Youlande Harrowell (Assistant Head Teacher). They have set up Mindful Equity UK, an organisation aiming to increase the representation of Black and minority ethnic teachers in leadership, when only 1% of UK Head Teachers are Black. We stand proudly with them and so many others, who have come forward to support and learn from each other. We hope, with all our hearts, that at least one person will find, in the following pages, a moment of recognition, as we did in our first meetings. In the words of Mayleen Atima, 'You are not alone.'

CHAPTER 1
I'm not Aunty, I'm your teacher

Ama Osapanin MCCT (Member of the Chartered College of Teaching)

Figure 1.1 Ama Osapanin

Figure 1.2 Ama and her dad

Growing up in central London was a lot of fun and a great experience! My parents made sure that my reality was safe and felt fair. I was a confident child, able to achieve whatever I set my heart on. A childhood full of strong role models definitely readied me for my path to leadership!

I attended a primary and secondary school that I have such fond memories of. I had teachers that were fun, supportive, motivating and inspiring. Often role models! Gosh, I hope I've had the same impact as a teacher!

As lovely as it all was, there are some memories of school that still don't make sense. Comments from teachers that weren't so positive; feedback that left me confused.

I remember at school, writing a recount for a piece of literacy homework. It was a simple enough task. I wrote about my weekend. A weekend that I had spent with family. I wrote about what we watched on the television; the songs that we sang at the top of our lungs, as my older cousin played an accompaniment on the piano; the food that we cooked and ate. My aunt taught me how to make hand-rolled noodles that weekend. We had a great time. A weekend I was happy and proud to be writing about. I was so motivated by this piece of work. Well, until my teacher marked it and gave it back to me.

The gist of the feedback was that my recount didn't sound very realistic and that people didn't hand-roll noodles. What? Erm, it was a completely accurate recount – thank you very much. And yes, in the Filipino village that my mother and aunt grew up in, people, sometimes, hand-rolled noodles. Skillfully too! It was a tradition that I loved learning and happily wrote about! But somehow, perhaps, it was too different an experience to be valued. Or, maybe, just too flamboyant for the assumptions that teacher had of me? Who knows?

My teacher told me that 'over here' people 'don't do that'. What? People don't spend time with their families? Of course they do! Were my family strange for being 'different' in the way that they spent that time? Were our weekend activities not good enough? Why wasn't I told that it sounded like a lovely weekend? That's what I wanted to hear.

I really didn't like how that felt. I was deflated. A little embarrassed too. Those questions. That doubt. It taught me to be less forthcoming about my experiences. I was a child, so I don't want to blame myself for not making a fuss at the time. But goodness me, now, as an adult and a teacher, I'd hate to think that children are still exposed to such ignorance.

When I told my mother that I wanted to be a teacher, she was delighted. It's a bit of a family tradition and I had no idea! It turns out that she was a primary school teacher in the Philippines. Before she came to England, in the 1960s, my mother was a primary school teacher. I couldn't believe it! She talked for a while about the age groups that she taught and the school that she worked in. Mum looked so happy in that moment of nostalgia. I asked why she didn't work as a teacher when she came to London. Well, that opened up a conversation about immigration and we went off on a tangent from there.

I had an almost identical conversation with my father! He, too, had been a teacher before he came to England. For years, he taught in primary and secondary schools across Ghana. Just like my mother, my father was filled with nostalgia as he spoke about his career in education. Again, I questioned why he didn't work as a teacher when he came to London. His response highlighted inequalities that left me with quite mixed feelings.

I was stuck on a thought for a while. I'd never seen a teacher that looked like me. Or my mum. Or my dad. By the time I had started university and was on teaching placements, that thought was a sad reality. One that I really didn't like. There was a complete lack of cultural representation at three out of the four schools where I completed a placement. I felt very aware of that and it was disappointing.

In the first term of my NQT year, a parent asked to meet me. They were upset that their child had been in trouble that week. That child had missed some of their playtime as a consequence of their behaviour. The parent was unhappy about this and, during a rant, told me that I was probably too strict because of my African upbringing!

Erm, no. That's not why I'm able to follow the school's behaviour system, but thanks for the insult. Thanks for the blatant racism! None of that was my actual response. I don't know what my response was, to be honest. I was so shocked and upset, I just wanted to run off and cry.

I mentioned it to a colleague and they laughed. They thought it was hilarious. I didn't mention it to anyone else. I should have said something. At least have informed my leadership team. But I felt really stupid and didn't want anyone else laughing at me.

In that first term, I wasn't really sure what to say and what to ignore. I didn't want to be accused of making a fuss. That wouldn't have happened. They wouldn't have laughed at me. The leadership team were brilliant and eventually I knew that I had their support. But knowing that took a while, so I said nothing. I felt alone.

Now, as a member of the leadership team, I feel more confident in general and especially in confronting comments that shouldn't be made. I am a valued member of my school community and have a great working relationship with colleagues and parents.

I can only remember one occasion in the last few years, where I feel like an offensive comment was made. I had phoned a new parent to arrange a home visit as their child was joining my school. We had a lengthy conversation and I answered the many questions they had about the school day and expectations.

I met that parent for the first time when I conducted the home visit. When I introduced myself, she told me that I looked different from what she was expecting. I asked her how I 'looked' different over the phone. It was an awkward moment and she muffled a pitiful explanation for what she meant. Hmmm … how, in the 21st century, can someone assume your voice has a specific skin tone?

Being, looking or feeling different isn't something to be ashamed of. We all know that! Sometimes it's nice to have a gentle reminder though. This last anecdote still makes me smile and is a great reminder!

Years ago, when teaching in the early years, a child refused to call me by my teacher name. To him, I looked like his aunties. And so, he called me Aunty! Did I mind? Not at all! Did he call any other member of staff Aunty? No. Did I like it? Yes! I loved that he saw a connection to his home life, in his new school setting, and used it to make that transition to school more comfortable for him. It made me smile knowing that I, by the way I looked, made that child feel like he was at home. Happy, safe and relaxed! Was he ready to learn? Yes! Did he stop calling me Aunty? Yes, eventually!

I've spent a few weeks asking myself why I have only shared these stories with my new group of colleagues. Well, this group feels different. I instantly felt part of something driving change. A community of people that I wanted to share my thoughts and experiences with.

Leaders for Race Equality has been a game-changer for me. We have so many shared stories. It's hard for me to talk openly about an experience, especially one that involves racism, without worrying that someone will try to unpick it. Somehow invalidate how I felt or what I thought. There's always that panic that I'll be expected to justify my reaction. Explain why I'm so offended. That's probably why I fell into the trap of saying nothing. But saying nothing changes nothing.

I know that now, and I have the confidence these days, to confront those situations. But as a Newly Qualified Teacher, I didn't have that confidence. For years, as a class teacher, I didn't either. I naively thought that no one could relate to how I felt. It's a weird thing to feel like no one really knows how you feel.

I was wrong to be embarrassed and ashamed by these awkward experiences, but who really tells themselves that in the moment? I didn't. It's refreshing to talk about something that

I've experienced in my career, and hear others say that they have too. It's a shame that we have negative experiences in common, but it's a huge comfort and a reminder that I'm not alone. It really is important to have a group that is invested in supporting every member.

I am grateful to be part of a professional network with so much to offer. We celebrate each other's achievements. That's not unusual, of course it isn't, but it does feel different when you know that someone else has faced similar challenges and ugly bias.

There have been a number of promotions within the group lately and it's a wonderful thing to be celebrating! It's not a smug celebration or a simple victory. It somehow, ever so slightly, feels like a shared journey. The idea to get where the others are in the group fills me with such hope and confidence but I'm not quite there yet. But it is where I definitely aspire to be!

CHAPTER 2

Changing the narrative

How I transformed labels into opportunities for growth and forged my own path

Danielle Lewis-Egonu

Figure 2.1 Danielle Lewis-Egonu

I thought it was best to set the context to give you, the reader, an idea of who I am and what I am about.

Why is this important?

Because this chapter is about labels, something I am often reduced to and this has become one of the deepest root causes to many of our problems as a British society. Labels hold a lot of meaning and are, therefore, quite dangerous. Since they are related to judgements, they can create stereotypes, hearsay, bias, fears, stigma and the inability to separate a person from the label itself.

I will lay all my labels out on these pages, in the hope that you derive a greater understanding of the why. Also, to offer the reasons behind what I have lived through in my career.

My experiences of covert and overt racism are entrenched in my earliest memories in both my experiences of the educational institution and interactions in society.

I was born in Camden in the 1980s.

My mum is White.

My half-sister, who I grew up with, is White.

My nanny, my uncles, my aunties and pretty much everyone I met, were White.

I had no Black role models, as I did not grow up with my father, who is of African-Caribbean descent and was part of the Windrush generation, who came to the United Kingdom between 1948 and 1970 from the Caribbean Islands, to help fill post-war UK labour shortages.

I did not realise I was brown until I was about 7, which may sound strange, but it's true.

No-one had told me I was Black and different. My mum took me to the park, the dentist and the doctors like all other mums did. My sister teased me and played with me just like any other sibling would. Of course, I had seen myself in the mirror many times, but I had not been labelled yet. It was just me and my family. The world had not decided, up until this point, that I needed to know I was brown.

It was only when I was playing one day in my primary school playground, on the ramp outside the dinner hall, with my good friend George that I began to make a connection with some of the situations I had encountered.

George stopped playing 'had' and told me that I could not play with him and his cousin anymore.

I was slightly confused as we played all the time inside and outside of school because our mums knew each other very well.

He told me I had to play with the other Black kids, and he could only play with the White kids and then tried to spit at me with his cousin, Tommy.

To say that this was distressing would be an understatement and when I told my mum, she said many words, which I cannot write in this piece, but needless to say that was the end of my friendship with George. We occasionally bumped into each other whilst we were growing up, but I would cross the street if I saw him.

He grew up and joined the National Front, who would proceed to regularly march on the streets that I called home, with the British flag as their symbol. When the IRA bomb went off on Camden High Street in February 1993, I momentarily thought it was planted by the NF to kill us, us Black people. The fear and trauma that the National Front had bestowed upon me was so great that I felt relieved when I found out it was another terrorist group who had caused the unforgivable pain and distress to the Camden community.

Something clicked when I realised that I was different to my family. I began to awaken to the fact that people would comment on my skin tone and would always ask who I belonged to or where I had come from, if I was out with my mum or sister. People felt they had the entitlement to question my existence and interrogate me because of the way I looked compared to my family. They would quite happily call me a liar and state that what I told them could not be true. How could it? How could a White family have a brown child unless I was adopted from a faraway land? It was unfathomable to many people, as there was no representation of families like mine anywhere.

My nanny quite happily dragged me to the Pie and Mash shop, which sat under the Camden Town Railway bridge on Royal College Street, for my serving of liquor and mash that I happily enjoyed, alongside my White family members. Yes, the place would fall silent when we came in. Yes, I got many looks from the people chomping on their meals, as I sat down for my favourite dish, as many would have been a part of the National Front. But my nanny did not care, I belonged to her, brown skin or not, because I was one of the 'good ones'; I was her granddaughter.

Ironically, we hardly ever talked about race in my family, but on one occasion, not long after the incident with George, when my mother did address it, she taught me that no-one would accept me. I was too dark to be accepted as White, too light to be accepted as Black and thus began the torment of finding my place in the world.

And sadly, for a long time, her teachings proved correct. 'Lightie, red girl, caramel sweetie, and bounty' are some of the names I was called over the years.

I became resilient.

I became used to racial abuse.

I became ready to enter the education institution, as a practitioner.

Why is my past relevant?

Because I faced the same abuse in my working life.

I am regularly reminded of my skin colour and how my very presence can offend because of it.

I have been spat at and worse, and told I do not belong.

I have felt the anger of my loved ones and my colleagues who have wanted to protect me from the world, but realise that they are powerless. They have heard the stories of how I have been treated for simply doing my job and have said words in frustration and sorrow, which I cannot repeat on these pages.

I have held parent meetings with terrorist group members that have caused me unforgivable pain and distress.

And I am still regularly interrogated by people who question my existence in education and whether I am entitled to be here, as they think I am a liar and a fraud. There are many meeting rooms I have walked into, which have fallen silent due to me being the only brown person there.

Society has labelled me a Black woman and imposed lots of judgement and stereotypes upon me due to this.

But the label I like best is the one my mum gave me: Danielle.

Danielle stands for a multi-layered individual, who loves her children, partner and family. She is intelligent, and conscientious and works in an institution where she belongs and offers representation, where the Google algorithm doesn't.

She is a great leader who offers clarity, focus and sensitivity whilst also loving innovation. She loves long walks, peanut butter milkshakes and Lake Como.

I just happen to be Black and sadly for many people that's all I will ever be.

Experiencing discrimination can provoke stress responses similar to post-traumatic stress disorder and therefore BAME staff need to feel supported by leadership in their school. The negative treatment affects an individual's life and wellbeing.

Early in my career I was spat at, harassed and verbally abused on a daily basis because my skin colour was hated. I would collect my class every day and brace myself for the abuse. I worked in an area where the British National Party were one of the majority parties in 2006. I dreaded every morning.

Trauma is an emotional response to a terrible event

I was experiencing this event daily and as a result I had a physical and emotional response to the trauma I was encountering and it could have ended my career before it had even begun.

I was the only Black staff member at the school, so staff hadn't experienced racism before and had no idea how to deal with it.

So, when my Head Teacher found me having a panic attack in the hallway one morning before collecting my class, she was quite confused when I told her what had been happening.

She had never made a connection between the impact of the BNP being elected and having a Black teacher; why would it be on her radar?

However, her response was the right one. She decided to educate herself and seek to understand.

She apologised for not noticing the morning issues.

She took a stand and made sure the parents knew what the expectations of their behaviour were in her school towards all of her staff.

She called the police and reported a hate crime (before hate crimes were taken seriously).

She came out into the playground with me every day until I felt safe enough to go out on my own again.

She didn't stop there.

She looked at representation in the curriculum, the staff and the environment because she started to see colour and that colour and difference was something to be celebrated and not a thing to be blind to.

There are many influences and experiences that have brought me to the point I am in my career today.

I am thankful that I never gave up and that I had company on the journey.

CHAPTER 3
My leadership journey

Debbie Doherty

Figure 3.1 Debbie Doherty

'I'm going be a teacher one day, Mum. You just wait and see!'

I was reported to have said to my mother as we walked to school one day, when I was about six years old.

I have no recollection of saying this. Perhaps I knew all those years ago the direction my career was going to take.

Growing up in an ethnically diverse suburb of the UK's second city and attending a primary school where the pupil demographic reflected this, stood in stark contrast to the single-sex grammar secondary school I attended, at which I first experienced explicit racism in the form of name-calling.

16   DOI: 10.4324/9781003498612-4

I was called the 'N' word by a girl who was three years my senior. I elected only to report this incident to my sister, who happened to be in the same year group as the perpetrator. She managed the situation on my behalf.

Moving to university was an exciting experience, though also daunting, because I was a bit of a 'mummy's girl'. I studied French and recall vividly sitting in a lecture theatre when I was asked to pronounce a French word aloud; 'le brouhaha'. As with my secondary school days, I was not particularly comfortable speaking or reading aloud. The lecturer could sense my discomfort, but insisted nonetheless. I refused and subsequently took the matter to the Head of Department who was 'not surprised' by the lecturer's approach. Indeed, it could have been that I was randomly selected; however, back then and for the first time, I felt that his insistence that I spoke came from a place of victimisation. I felt targeted. On reflection, the word was not that difficult to pronounce.

On embarking on my teacher training back in 1990, I had yet another unpleasant experience. I needed some 'digs' for the year I would spend completing my PGCE. I saw an advert on the campus, visited the house, which was owned by a lovely elderly lady, agreed rent, moving in date, and so on. I returned a few weeks later, rang the bell and my soon-to-be landlady appeared and promptly informed me that the deal was off. In complete shock and disbelief, I asked why. Quite courageously I guess, she proceeded to tell me that her son had advised her against renting the room to someone like me. My student status was not the issue; my skin colour was. Every cloud has a silver lining however, as a week later I rented a room from one of the (White) college lecturers who I subsequently and ever since have referred to as my surrogate mum. We remained friends and in contact until she died in 2017. I still keep in contact with her daughter, son and husband – my surrogate sister, brother and dad.

Pursuing leadership roles was not on my agenda in my early teaching career. I was more than happy being a classroom teacher in the middle school I joined as a Newly Qualified Teacher in Milton Keynes in 1991. Looking back on my career (and life) as a whole, I realise now that I had been very naïve and had probably experienced many implicit incidences of racism. Conversely, for the most part, I do not think that the colour of my skin has hindered my career progression. I was a good classroom practitioner and soon found that my qualities were recognised and rewarded. After a few years, I was given a management role (does anyone remember Management points, the precursor to Threshold?). I was offered the role of mentor to students and rose to Deputy Head after several years. I was fortunate enough to gain secondment experiences in two settings, one as an Acting Deputy in a very challenging school at that time, the second being a two-term Acting Head secondment at a local first school which was extended to two years.

From a career development perspective, my tenure at that school was very rewarding. I successfully built excellent relationships with the children, parents and the wider community (especially the bakery opposite the school, the perfect place to indulge my love for all things sweet). Relationships, both professional and personal, were equally positive with staff … except one. My high expectations of all staff (including myself) coupled with my visionary approach was met with disdain. Am I sure this was a consequence of my management style? No, I am not, but who knows? Despite this, during my time at the same school I experienced positive discrimination. The city was on a serious recruitment drive and along with an older male White Head Teacher in the city, I was asked to be 'the face of Milton Keynes'. The photo shoot went ahead. On receiving the phone call about enlisting my services, I enquired why I had been selected. I knew the answer, but instead I asked if I had been selected because of my beautiful smile (which is true incidentally). In doing so, was I indirectly trying to shield her embarrassment? In short, this was positive discrimination. In 2020 speak, that's inclusion. Nothing wrong with that. I adopted the same approach when recently putting together a virtual tour of my school. The camera zoomed in on the photos of the staff who are also ethnically diverse. Children of different ethnicities were also represented. As people from minority ethnic groups, ever more so today, it's essential to be able to identify with others, at school age and beyond. The expression 'you can't be what you can't see' resonates here.

At the end of that secondment period, I returned to my previous school to assume the role of Interim Head whilst the school recruited for a permanent role. It was during that year that I saw a very different side to two particular members of the governing board, people who I had known for many years, people who were very much aware of the contribution I had made to the school. In the 'boardroom' decisions, strategies were challenged more than they ever had been. The trusting and supportive approach, which I had enjoyed for many years, was no more. I felt very much undermined. Was it a gender issue? Unlikely. Was it a race-related micro-aggression? Perhaps? Who knows? Needless to say, I didn't apply for the substantive post. It wouldn't have worked; I needed and wanted to move on. Looking back, I wish I had the courage to openly challenge the opposition. I'm in a much stronger place emotionally now.

I actively sought other positions and was shortlisted. I have been lucky to have been shortlisted for all positions I have applied for, except the International School in New York (what was I thinking??!!). One particular role, which would have been my first substantive headship, I didn't secure. I wasn't that disappointed. Unknowingly, it paved the way for my next move.

If I were to offer you advice or words of wisdom, I would say this: racism is systemic, but if you are unsuccessful in securing a leadership role, don't immediately assume that it's because of implicit, explicit racial discrimination although, as we are acutely aware, that may well be the case. In my experience, it has been about the right fit. Why else would I have secured my first substantive post in a semi-rural primary school where I was the only staff member of colour, where 99% of the pupil population were White British and where the village itself had, I believe, less than a handful of residents of colour. I had an amazing experience; I learnt my craft and even though I say it myself, I was well respected by the pupils, staff, parents and governors.

Despite all this positivity, the local village shopkeeper showed her true colours on one occasion when I went on an official errand (I don't quite recall the reason but it was a task which my administrator would ordinarily have done). We didn't have ID badges at that school (yikes, I hear you all cry) but to cut to the end of the story, the interaction that ensued demonstrated that the shop assistant did not believe I could possibly have been the Head Teacher of the school.

A similar situation presented itself when my long-time friend, who is White, invited me to her school in Hertfordshire to help deliver some materials on the subject of the Windrush years. I invited my (White) Deputy to accompany me for some personal CPD, looking simply at different classroom practices. Needless to say, on arrival the staff assumed that my Deputy was the Head Teacher. Perfect example of unconscious bias. Or was it due to my youthful looks, which caused them to think it was impossible for me to hold such a position? Over 15 years later, I am told I still look younger than my years. I am grateful to my mother and grandmother for my genes.

As you may have noticed, there are numerous 'who knows?' questions in my story. The truth of the matter is, I guess in some instances, I will never know for sure and as none of it has been an obstacle to my career progression, I reflect and view the less than supportive people I encountered along the way as simply uninformed, unknowing, exposing their unconscious (or conscious) bias.

I was interviewed on BBC Northampton Radio about three years ago, on my role in education and my experiences of racism. The interviewer was pushing me to share any racist experiences. I struggled to think of anything specific at the time and concluded that, actually, my journey had been overwhelmingly positive. It is, however, the topical events of late which have forced me to review my career, and only now have I removed this cloak of naivety and taken the time to explore past events, not in the search of being able to categorise them as racist, but just to review them with my eyes wide open. My experience has indeed been overwhelmingly positive. I realise, though, that that is not the case for all.

So, whilst this story gives you an insight into my professional life, the poem below (composed in 2017 as part of my school's World Book Day activities) may give you a flavour of my other, perhaps most important part.

I come from ...

I come from… 3 siblings, all older, making me the baby of the family,

I come from… rice and peas, chicken with home-made coleslaw on the side, curry goat and Saturday soup,

I come from………. a Jamaican village and a Jamaican city, even though I have never been,

I come from…………. loving school from the age of 5 to the age of 18 and actually enjoying doing homework,

I come from…………. playing Charlie's Angels and Knock Down Ginger on the street where I lived as a child,

I come from…………… 'Holby City' and 'Casualty', my favourite TV series,

I come from………….. naming my cars Belinda, Selina and Mariah,

I come from………….. high aspirations and believing in myself, thanks to my mum,

But most importantly, I come from Melissa and Edward (daughter and husband); we are the 3 Musketeers!

CHAPTER 4
Best fit

Diana Ohene-Darko

Figure 4.1 Diana Ohene-Darko

Primary school was where I first experienced 'race'. Since we were a Catholic family, my twin sister and I attended the local Catholic primary school; some 250 pupils of mainly White-British and White-Irish ethnicity. Compare this to the handful, if that, of children who were not White: one boy who was Black, another set of twins who were Indian and a girl who had both Black and White heritage.

From the outset I could 'see' the disparity – large numbers of children and all the adults with a different skin tone and life experience to mine. We were an immigrant family – expelled under the Idi Amin regime in the early 1970s. Second generation. My parents and older siblings had suffered through that turmoil, and arrived in this country with just the clothes on their backs. My late father came ahead of them to secure housing and transfer with his job.

Fast forward to the 1980s when racism in Britain was in its prime and no 'brown' person escaped unscathed. 'Paki' was a common term used back then for most foreigners, no matter if they were Pakistani or not. I always felt different. I wasn't into the same things as the other girls. I always felt like I should be; why wasn't I? I couldn't wait to leave primary school, not least because I knew there was a big, wide world out there and I was stuck in a corner of it.

Cue 1990s and high school. This was an absolute gift of experience and identity-belonging; or not as the case may be. Cliques gathered on the playgrounds, each with their own specified territory. Woe-betide anyone who dared take it. Each space had an unsaid rule about the occupancy. Having a Goan father and a White-British mother, I was not part of any visible groups. I couldn't fit in with the all-Whites, or the all-Asians. There were very few children, if any, of mixed heritage of my own or a similar ethnicity. The go-to term for us was 'half-caste', a term I never understood because I wasn't Indian and so wasn't part of the 'Caste System'. High school was met with a mixture of friends from different backgrounds, an often lonely and hard-to-navigate time in terms of fitting in and having that sense of belonging. Thank goodness I always had my twin sister with whom I already had a well-established sense of identity and belonging. What I did realise in these years was that I had an inherent and deep-rooted sense of justice and equality. Learning about prejudice and discrimination in Religious Education spurred me on to find out more and do my own research. I found myself watching films such as *Mississippi Burning* and *Cry Freedom*, *Roots* even, to try and gain some context and background to the education that I received in school. I relished my learning – the empowerment and veneration of Black and Indian leaders (namely Martin Luther King Jr and Mahatma Gandhi) gave me hope for a better, more equal world; one where I could fit in and also one where I could advocate for justice. My innate will for equality was ignited. I felt it then and I still feel it now.

Fast forward to university and I had a similar experience to primary school; one main ethnicity and a deep feeling of being the odd one out. I have made my closest friends as an adult, yet none of them resemble my own background. We are a flavoursome array of heritages, beliefs and traditions. And I wouldn't have it any other way.

When training to be a teacher, I undertook the Graduate Teacher Programme (GTP) as it was then. I fell into teaching by first becoming a Teaching Assistant and absolutely loved it. I loved being with the children and igniting that flame of learning; helping them through challenging tasks and developing their character. At long last, by the age of 25, I knew this was my vocation.

Whilst still training, I was given class responsibility, which was unheard of at the time. It felt as though my innate dynamism as a teacher and passion for education had been understood from the outset by leaders already in the field. I took great pride in setting up my classroom, organising tables and a seating plan, my desk and personal items. Before long, I was in the swing of the weekly timetable and teaching all subjects whilst finishing my course. At first the regular pop-ins/observations/stay in class sessions didn't seem too untoward. I had to have weekly observations anyway as part of the course. It wasn't until a table was set up in an unused classroom opposite, where two teachers 'set up shop' so to speak, that I began to feel very uneasy; targeted even. They remained there for a full term, which was the duration of my course. Neither teacher was in class; they took groups every now and then but other than that I'm not sure what they did, other than observe my every move. I continued with profound enthusiasm for the children I had in front of me. Nothing gave me greater pleasure than those light-bulb moments in which children 'got it'. I even took the liberty of re-creating Jane Ellis' blue-eye/brown-eye experiment as part of a discrimination lesson in RE. I was creative, confident and always maintained a positive outlook. Perhaps that's what got to them. I passed my course with flying colours and went on to complete my Newly Qualified Teacher year, again in Year 6, before completing a year in Year 4. I built up my experience of teaching (and courage) before moving onto to my first leadership position for a curriculum area, with oversight over the whole curriculum.

My next assignment was an academy, an altogether corporate experience, dripping in wealth I had never known as part of a local authority school. It was good to have the luxury of IT technicians on demand, a healthy budget to spend on trips and resources and to be able to move between year groups, given the chance. Here I learned the valuable lessons of real team work (working with a partner teacher, as it was two-form entry) and the progression of an all-through school (Nursery to Sixth Form). By becoming involved in family learning, I saw a different side to education, enjoying the partnerships between school and families. I also had the opportunity to teach in Reception, one of my most treasured years in teaching. What an insight and indeed privilege to be part of the picture at such a young age – teaching children to do up their zips, put on their PE kits, read and much more! Perhaps because I had young children of my own, I understood the cherished position I was in, helping these little people to confidently grow and learn. I loved those days. There was a song for everything and for everything there was a song! That was my motto.

Tensions were rife that year among middle and senior leaders. The Senior Leadership Team (SLT) was made up of one ethnicity and it was clear that no one else would make it through. I took another bold decision to move on. This time to a more senior post, taking on responsibility for Literacy in a Junior school. I would be part of the SLT.

Have you ever wondered if you fit the bill? Are you the right (acceptable) colour? Do you speak (acceptably) well? I'm a light shade of brown, olive skin some might say. I speak well, pronouncing my 't's and 'f's correctly. I'm an acceptable shade it would seem. But I know colleagues who have not been afforded the same recognition. Nothing is ever said of course but 'best fit' often wins the day after interview.

This school was different. Under a leadership of resolute equality and diversity, I never once questioned my place or position, my experience or even my background. I felt completely valued for who I was and the different perspective I sometimes brought. I took great pride when I was assigned to lead Global Links and the Rights Respecting Schools Award (RRSA). These became my babies, professionally. I put my heart and soul into them. I was then part of a sensational team of staff from admin to TAs, teachers to the site supervisor who equally nurtured and championed the RRSA and our global partnership into life. We lived and breathed children's rights, taking our role as duty-bearers seriously and by taking part in events such as WE day, annual fundraisers (skip-a-thon, no screen day, dance-a-thon) and reciprocal visits to our link school in Uganda (which I had set up as part of a trip I undertook with a charity). I can't tell you the difference it makes working with such leadership and a team of people who are like-minded. I had complete autonomy in my roles and was trusted implicitly because I always had the best interests of the children and families at the heart of what I did. What an honour to have led this initiative and to have learned under this leadership. My career is so much the better for it and so am I. With more than a decade under this leadership I learned a lot about who I wanted to be, and who I am, as a leader. Kindness, compassion and empathy go a long way. So too does integrity – who are you when no one is watching?

Currently, I am on the path to headship. Having made two applications, one was rejected straight off (faith school for which I had no current leadership experience) and the other I made it to the last two with lots of positives to take away and a couple of things to work on. I was left with the question as to whether I want a Head of School post or a Head Teacher post. I know now that I firmly want the latter. I want to be part of the next generation of leaders; leaders who have equality on the agenda; leaders who 'see' everyone and are bold enough to make changes. I want to be that change. I want to make a difference. I want to leave a small part of the world better than I found it.

To those entering the profession or seeking leadership: go confidently into your future. Be bold, be brave and be you. Who you are will make the difference.

CHAPTER 5
Challenging times

Elaine Williams

Figure 5.1 Elaine Williams

The early days were the hardest. I never imagined that securing my first job would be so difficult. Good degree classification, very strong school experiences. Phrases like, 'she's a natural', 'so talented', 'highly employable' were phrases that I had become accustomed to. I was young, no ties, so confidently applied for jobs up and down the country.

I was willing to teach anywhere! Each rejection, and there were many, dulled my shine a little bit. But I was nothing if not resilient, so I continued to bounce back. I'm not going to lie, travelling over 200 miles, on public transport, only to be told that it was close but it had gone to somebody older, hurt. My age was on the application form, the thing that wasn't on the application form was my colour. My name didn't give that sneak preview, which was obviously desired. It was simply not possible to act on the post interview feedback I was consistently given: too young, not enough experience, nothing you could change, someone just pipped you to it. These statements were all useless to me. All they did was start to reinforce an idea I was having that people didn't want black teachers. There was no space for us in British schools. It hurt. I felt that I had been lied to. Why let me spend time completing a teaching degree if I'd never be good enough to secure a job? Why grade me so highly on assignments and school experiences if I'd never get a chance to have my own class?

I had applied for so many that when I was called for an interview to a school in Dewsbury, Yorkshire, I couldn't even remember applying for it. It was a part-time post (I needed full time work but like I said, I applied for anything). I didn't get it. It went to a Punjabi speaker. That I completely understood, especially given the catchment area. They told me my interview was strong. It was simply that the successful candidate had that 'dual language' edge. I understood. They offered me two weeks' work instead. They needed someone to cover a member of staff who was ill. I accepted. I had to start somewhere. Five years later, I was still at that school. I gained a wealth of experience. I was nurtured, developed and constantly told that I was a leader of the future. Every cloud.

My first headship. I think I sort of fell into that. Don't get me wrong, I knew I wanted to be a Head Teacher, it was all part of my plan, but the chain of events was strange. I was a Deputy in Leeds. I thought that perhaps I should get a little more leadership experience in a different school before applying for my first headship. My Head laughed, she said I was selling myself short and that I was ready for headship. I flicked through the *Times Ed* and saw a headship advertised, local to my hometown. I knew nothing about the school. I didn't expect to get an interview and if I secured an interview, I felt that they would give me actions to work on as part of feedback. When they called to offer me the job, I was speechless. This was not how I had planned things would work out.

So there I was, Head Teacher of a small, rural primary school. I was the only black person there; no other black staff, no black children. The environment was a change for me but we were a community. Although it was hard work (small school challenges, nothing to do with ethnicity), I loved it.

I continued in this post for approximately four years. I knew I wanted a different challenge and my journey took me to the West Midlands. In my mind, this would be a positive move. I was moving to a multi-cultural metropolis. I was expecting to be welcomed with open arms by the staff and the parents. This was my experience in my first headship, so why would it not be even better, in a multi-cultural environment? I was excited, nervous, yes, but excited. I'd left my previous school with letters of thanks from the parents, governors and staff. The local authority had also written to me congratulating me on my success in running the school and serving the school community so well. I was proud and honoured to have made a difference, and for that difference to be recognised and celebrated.

Yorkshire was an instrumental part in my leadership journey. Yes, I worked for different local authorities throughout this time, but in both of them I felt that the school communities I worked in saw me and wanted me. There was a clear desire for me to be their leader, respect was paramount. They valued everything I brought to the table. I'll never know if they saw me as a black leader or a leader who happened to be black. What I do know is they saw me as a successful leader and that enabled me to continue to grow, develop and refine my practice. It was miles away from the early rejection days when I struggled to secure that first post.

The West Midlands. Remembering some of the challenges makes my heart sink. Then I remind myself that leadership is like a rollercoaster. With that rollercoaster comes the inevitable ups and downs. It was never going to be easy running a school where the Deputy had also applied for the headship, and clearly had been unsuccessful, as the job was mine. You learn something about the application process with each interview. For my next one I would check that there were no internal applicants, but I didn't know about this one until I'd accepted the post. I had developed a thick skin over the years, so deep breathing and counting to ten served me well. Headship can be a lonely place but when your Deputy refuses to even say hello to you, let alone work with you, it's a very challenging situation.

There were times when I honestly felt very sorry for the staff. They were caught between a rock and a hard place. The two Senior Leaders were not working together and were clearly not on the same page. When the Deputy secured a new Deputy position, it was like a weight was lifted off my shoulders. Now that that barrier was removed, I could continue to move the school forward. I knew what good leadership looked like, but I soon learnt that new barriers could be put in your way, at any given moment. The thing that upsets me most about the barriers encountered in this post is the fact that, I believe, they were due to my colour. This shouldn't have been happening in this day and age. It was also surprising it was happening in a 'multi-cultural' environment.

I was often in a no-win situation. Parents, staff, it was hard! There were times when that rollercoaster crashed right down to the bottom, and I was not screaming because I was enjoying the ride.

I was told by White parents that I was racist. I was 'all for the Black children' and I 'don't care about the White ones'. They said that I gave the Black children preferential treatment and I was unfairly hard on the White children. I was accused of racism by the Black parents. They said that I 'didn't understand Black children' and that I had 'sold out' because I only cared about the White children. They said I was 'too hard' on the Black children. No win. As a leader, you take each situation and manage each one within the policies and procedures you have in place. It's never about colour, but that was a battle I just couldn't win.

Staff. Some staff were great and really kept me going. Others … they didn't want me there. They would do anything to see me fail, and try anything to make leave. Dark days.

I can remember one member of staff contacting the police in order to tell them that I was allowing weed on the premises. Yep, she wanted to damage my reputation and career that much. Obviously there was no truth in it and nothing happened as a result of this, but someone said that about me, when I'm sure they wouldn't have said it about a White Head Teacher.

Another member of staff, who clearly thought it was time for me to move on, found and showed me new Head Teacher positions. Who does this for their Head Teacher? She obviously didn't want to risk coming across me again as all the posts were international, in fact, they were in the Caribbean. I'm guessing that wouldn't have happened to a White Head Teacher.

I did move on eventually, but I moved on when it was right for me. I was not going to be forced to move because of other people. Nobody knows how leadership positions will work out. You can research and ask questions but nobody has a crystal ball. Just know that once that rollercoaster hits the bottom, it has to go back up at some point.

I'm still in the West Midlands and, although my new post it had its challenges when I started, they weren't about race or ethnicity. I have been told recently that my school is diverse, both in terms of the children and families who are part of the school community and the staff who work within the school. This is something of which I am proud.

CHAPTER 6
It takes a village to raise a child

Lorna Legg

Figure 6.1 Lorna Legg

Figure 6.2 Lorna and her family

I don't think, if you'd asked me back in early childhood, that I'd have been able to tell you what colour I was, or anyone else for that matter. Until I was about eight years old, I don't think I'd have understood the question. Then, we moved house and an imposed identity I had been almost unaware of – race – became all pervasive, and coloured my days from then on. I left my happy, diverse, big town school in Northampton, to attend a small, local village primary school in Oxfordshire.

Here is where my little sister and I came face to face with a new and confusing parallel universe. Suddenly, how we looked, what we wore, even how we spoke, came under intense scrutiny, as with all new children, but their attentions were tinged with something negative and new. Rapidly, I began to feel, without knowing how or why, that I had said or done something wrong; in fact, it's more accurate to say that I began to feel, intrinsically, that everything about me was wrong. Several, initially incomprehensible comments were made about my sister and I needing a wash, or being 'dirty'.

I remember, for the first time, noticing that my knees were so much darker than theirs and so, at night in the bath, I would scrub them, until sometimes there were pinpricks of blood. I hoped my dark brown knees might fade, but of course, they never did. It has taken a long time to realise the fault did not lie in my skin, but in their response to it. My hair, too, which I'd never really thought about (unless Mum combed it; a task we faced with mutual dread), became something people would comment on, or want to touch. I just wanted to blend in, have long, silky hair, like the other girls, and have nobody ask me where I came from, because the honest answer – 'Northampton' – never seemed to be quite what they were after.

I became increasingly aware of how people of colour – any colour aside from White – were represented on television. Any positive role models, like Floella Benjamin and Derek Griffiths, on children's TV, or Daley Thompson triumphing in the Decathlon, would be watched in a state of painful hope. How they performed, I now realise, was so important to my developing self-image. Sadly, more often than not, the stereotypes we saw were harmful. A few of my new school 'mates' – not all, but enough – influenced by seventies TV perhaps, or possibly comments overheard at home, started to use names that are hard to write, but even harder to hear: stupid, childish names perhaps, but hurtful, because that was their intention.

As a child, when we went to any village event, my biggest fear was that this small, but significant group might call out those horrible names in front of my mum. I felt I might catch fire and die of shame if she heard, but I never, for a second, considered telling anyone. Why is it that this shame, which should rightfully have been theirs, affected me so much? So many children will have gone, and will go through, their own versions of this, including my own beautiful, kind children, who have both heard the 'N' word, from adults as well as children.

It wasn't until later in life that I learnt more about my own mother's struggles. Coming to 'The Mother Country', as she saw it, from Jamaica, leaving her own mother behind, must have taken all my mum's courage and hope. She left a place of warmth, love and beauty, to arrive on a damp, greasy dock, where everything (sky, ground, faces) seemed grey: drained of colour and joy. The elderly 'gentleman' who spat at her at a bus-stop, telling her to go back to where she came from, presumably didn't want her care, or that of the many overseas nurses who came to support the NHS.

Mum eventually won over my very English paternal grandmother; caring for her in her old age, even though Grandma initially tried to prohibit their marriage, back in the sixties, managing to prevent some family and friends from attending their wedding. How some people treated Mum was simply puzzling: pretending not to hear her greetings, avoiding eye contact, or turning away as if they hadn't seen her. Shop assistants would sometimes refuse to take money from her hand. The thing I could never work out, and cannot to this day, is that these people never seemed to see *her*: the kindest, gentlest and most generous person I have ever known. Despite all that she has experienced, this has never changed. With Dad still at her side almost 55 years later, their love, and her example, have been my saving grace. She endured a myriad of put-downs, yet rose to the top of her profession.

Now, as Head Teacher of a small village primary school, I have the opportunity to protect children; to prevent them from experiencing or participating in discrimination; to encourage our pupils to see the person, before everything else. Most teachers do their best to view others without prejudice, or at least understand they must try. However, before becoming a Head, I came across those who held prejudiced views. They could state things like 'Black people can't swim', as if fact, and who would insinuate that my rejection of such throw-away racial or sexist comments were simply indicative of a lack of humour, due to either my colour or my gender. In one school, I overheard Mealtime Assistants commenting on the fact a Reception child, who was Black, couldn't do up his laces ('Don't suppose they have shoes where he comes from'), ignoring the fact (until I pointed it out) that not a single other child of his age can, either. Therefore, while it may not always be explicit, or aggressive, racism persists in many forms, despite race being completely without scientific basis.

There are things I feel unable to share, which affected me deeply, but I know none of the experiences I have been through are, in themselves, knock-out blows – after all, here I am. I put any success down to my parents, three special teachers and an inner determination to show I could succeed, despite what others might think. My supportive husband, also a Head, happens to be both White and male. He has been lucky enough to have had only two interviews in his working life (also of 20 years) compared to my ten (plus) interviews. I do not claim that this is a representative sample, nor do I claim that all my failed interviews have been linked to prejudice around my ethnicity: maybe I can chalk a few down to sexism, many will have been down to my own failings and, to be fair, I learnt a lot from each rejection. However, the stigma associated with growing up, feeling that you are somehow wrong in some indefinable way, can be all-pervasive and fundamentally undermining, especially in the stress of an interview.

Mandatory, national training for governors and staff (preferably everyone) in implicit bias, would be a good place to start to redress any disadvantage and open up leadership to a more representative and diverse group of people. I am grateful to my Diocese, which supported a free, online session, and my local authority, which has, at least, put forward one session aimed at de-colonising the curriculum (although at a cost). The fact that the NAHT and other bodies are establishing groups like ours, to begin to address the issues we face, is clearly a start and I have found a sense of belonging in this group I have seldom felt before. However, these isolated attempts to fill a yawning gap in our education and that of our peers and pupils is not enough ... yet.

Unless our children have role models, in whom they can see themselves, are confident in their unique gifts and in the knowledge they are loved, and can share that love with others, society cannot thrive as it should. Racism, sexism and homophobia still consign too many of our young people to a future they do not deserve. For the future to truly be brighter, we need to shine a light on all the wrongs committed out of sight, teach ourselves and others to stand up for what is right, and learn to let our lights shine, undimmed.

Figure 6.3 Lorna's mum and dad

It takes a village to raise a child

Figure 6.4 Lorna and her mum

CHAPTER 7
All I ever wanted to be was a teacher

Mayleen Atima

Figure 7.1 Mayleen Atima

Figure 7.2 Mayleen's mum and dad

Since I was a little girl, all I ever wanted was to be was a teacher. My mother was a childminder and, inadvertently, it too became my first 'job'. The two children that my mum looked after plus my younger siblings became my first 'class'. They even received homework every day and if they did not complete it – detention!

I went to a secondary school in Brockley, south London, where gangs, underage sex and Class C drugs were the norm. However, peer pressure did not influence me, as I had a greater fear of my church-going Caribbean parents. I was one of ten children and the first to go to university.

Until attending university, I had never experienced any kind of overt racism.

My first experience was whilst standing at the bus-stop outside my university in Eltham, when a car came speeding up the road. Out of instinct, I jumped behind the glass partitioning, just before an egg splattered on the glass. A sobering event and I realised, in that particular area, it was not safe to walk around on my own. From then on my friend and I would wait for each other. There were only three Black people on our course and we could definitely feel all eyes were on us. A feeling that words cannot explain but we instinctively knew that we needed to stick together.

I made it to my final year of studying a BA English + Qualified Teacher Status. I had taken part in three successful teaching practices and had started my fourth and final practice. I was so excited, but by week five of my practice, I was failing. I had lost weight and most of my confidence. The teacher picked apart everything that I did. In one lesson when I was teaching PE, I tripped and fell. The teacher just looked at me; she did not attempt to help or offer any comfort. Other teachers would console me and tell me that I was doing a good job. However, I could not seem to get any recognition from this teacher. At the time, I did not think it was about the colour of my skin, but in hindsight what else could it have been? My mentor could not believe the change in my teaching and so I took a year out. The university allowed me to come back with no additional costs and retake my final practice to great success. I chalked this up to a bad experience and finally plucked up the courage to apply for my first teaching role.

I started as a Newly Qualified Teacher (NQT) in April 2001, at a church school in Greenwich, London. I was a year 1 teacher and very excited. There was one other NQT in the school and we soon became great friends. Her father was well-known in education circles, so when the time came for her to move into a leadership position within the school the door was open wide for her. However, I felt I was not ready. Therefore, I was happy for her and her ambition and content to stay in class to develop my teaching and leadership skills.

Some years later, my friend (who I will call Claire) got married. She went on maternity leave and I took over all her leadership roles, which included Special Educational Needs Coordinator. In addition, I was now managing Safeguarding, Computing, Music and Behaviour across the school. I was a member of the governing body and a lead teacher in the Friends of the School charity group. I was the DJ at every school disco and would stay until all the cleaning was completed. Moreover, my pupils were gaining good outcomes each year. I knew that I was good at my job, I had a natural flair for leadership and I loved it. During Claire's maternity leave, I decided that I should talk to the Head Teacher about temporarily making me part of the Senior Leadership Team in her absence. The Head Teacher refused and despite me sharing that I had taken over all her responsibilities but with no recognition, he continually refused to acknowledge my contributions.

I realised at that point that, within that school, I had come to the end of my career progression and attended a Deputy Head Teacher training course. I applied for several jobs and finally got an interview. The Head Teacher was shocked when he heard that I had an interview. He asked me for my personal statement so that he could write the reference. After reading the personal statement, he stated that it was full of grammatical errors and I should have let him read it before applying for the job. I was annoyed and my confidence was knocked. Deep down I knew that he did not want me to go, but still his words and actions hurt.

I went to my interview and got the job. At my new school, I met an amazing Head Teacher, who has now become one of my closest friends. Years later, she shared with me that when she called the Head Teacher from my previous school, she had to prompt him to give a verbal reference and that he was very tight-lipped.

I cried. Even though a few years had passed and I was thriving in my new school. The knowledge that he still refused to recognise my contributions to the school remained hurtful. I had moved on, but the pain remained.

In 2010, I became Deputy Head Teacher of a school in Southwark. This school had a number of Black and minority ethnic teachers, which I had never experienced before, so I was very excited. On my first day, the Head Teacher walked me around the school and introduced me to one of the Black teachers who was also a senior teacher. She sneered at me and said 'Do us proud' then walked away.

I went from feeling immense excitement to feeling a dead weight of expectation upon me. It proved to be a clear sign of what was to come. Over the next two years, my biggest protagonists were the Black and other minority ethnic teachers. I could not put a foot right and no matter what I did, they felt I was targeting them. Not only did I feel I had to prove myself to the school community, I also felt a pressure to prove myself to the Black teachers in my school. But I never gave up!

I am now an established Head Teacher in Suffolk, running a school that has improved from Requires Improvement to Good. All I ever wanted to be was a teacher and I have achieved that goal.

When I reflect on my journey, I realise that I used my struggles to become my victories.

The future Black leaders within education, I would like them to remember:

- You are not alone
- Never give up
- You have so much to offer
- You too can achieve your goals.

CHAPTER 8
Coming out BAME
Two moments

Rick Stuart-Sheppard

Figure 8.1 Rick Stuart-Sheppard

I attended a leadership group meeting for those of us who are Black, Asian and Minority Ethnic.

Wow.

How extraordinary it felt to be in the midst of education leaders who all shared a characteristic with me – that of not being White.

DOI: 10.4324/9781003498612-9 43

Rick Stuart-Sheppard

It was the first time in my professional life where I was part of a group where my ethnic minority identity put me in the majority.

I didn't say anything in the virtual meeting. It was enough to be present.

My journey to wholeness, completeness or acceptance of my identity has been lifelong and the moment of revelation was unexpected.

A few years previously, I was at our county Head Teacher's conference and the presenter was delivering a talk on the curriculum.

It concerned a country in Africa about which he cheerfully admitted he had known nothing. He had been hired to deliver some curriculum support and development to a school there and it was the night before he was to work with a teacher and he had arrived at the hotel. What to do? To the amusement from his audience of Head Teachers and leaders, he confessed to 'Googling' it.

And when he Googled it, he found out that the capital of this country was 'not safe after dark'. This was delivered almost as a piece of stand-up comedy, on some level, and the audience of my peers greeted it with laughter in all the right/wrong places. I was becoming increasingly agitated. My daughter was working in this country and I knew they were currently holding elections that had turned dangerous and violent. Beyond the photogenic wildlife, it had also produced the father of a recent American president. This president's father had taken some positives from the British rule of his country, before a hard-fought Independence had been gained.

How could it be possible to present your ignorance of even an acquaintance of British involvement in this country as something for mirthful entertainment?

How could you present your ignorance of a fact, which must surely be a piece of shared cultural capital, as something to share a laugh about? Soon there would be a break, and we would be drinking tea or coffee that stood a reasonable chance of having been produced and exported from this country of which he was claiming happily to know nothing. And, more infuriatingly, he was inviting us, as supposed educated leaders of education, to join him in laughing at our collective ignorance and dismissal of an entire nation, and one from which the British had directly ruled, shaped, manipulated and benefited.

I was spinning. Part of me wanted to stand up and denounce this madness, this wilful amnesia, swear aloud at the craziness of proclaiming ignorance of our shared history. As I struggled with this rage building inside, I looked around my table, the colleagues I had worked with, and I felt completely alone. They seemed to be with him, smiling. The room was with him.

I was the only person visibly 'not White' in the room. Years of telling myself that things were changing, the ethnic make-up of our schools were changing and soon our teachers and leaders would reflect this; I realised I had been misguided. I knew more was being asked of me now, because time alone was not going to address the issues that I couldn't even begin to formulate: invisible histories, unconscious bias and unseen privilege.

I spoke to him after, briefly, as calmly as I could, and he apologised, on some level. Perhaps I should say he attempted to defuse. My anger was all over the place: his presentation, his colleague trying to speak up for him, my peers around me and myself, for taking so long to get to this point and not knowing how to respond honestly, authentically and constructively. It was too big for me.

I went to find the guys selling Information Technology (IT), in the next room. They were the only other people present who, like me, were visibly 'non-White'.

The IT guys and I had met the night before.

'Guys, can I talk to you? … I am so angry and I don't know who I can talk to.'

They let the sales go for a few minutes to share their own story: expulsion from Uganda, their father's jute farm expropriated; resettlement in Britain.

They had come over, grown up, and were doing their best to make it work. It made it clear to me that there are hundreds of thousands, millions probably, of stories about how we come to be in Britain – each unique and personal. They are all connected to larger stories: how Britain ruled a certain place, how it left that place and what happened next.

An education system and curriculum that produces a (well remunerated?) key note speaker, who can make his ignorance of our shared history an amusing way in to a (highly paid?) gathering of school leaders – this is not a good situation. It 'Requires Improvement', at best.

The people who know and understand the actual history of this country and how we all come to be here were working the stalls, selling IT and cleaning the rooms.

It shook me, following so close upon major public events (Brexit) and deep personal events (my parents reaching the end of their lives).

My path has been as individual as any immigrant, taking in my father's departure from India after Independence, my mother leaving Australia in the Depression, and their joint decision that Canada would make a better place to bring up their family. I think they kept the specifics of their experiences as a 'Mixed' couple in Britain in the late 50s–early 60s silent and buried from us, trying to build a new life in a different country. Their reluctance to talk about ethnicity and their experiences as a 'Mixed-Race' couple seem, from where I am now, to have been an unspoken strategy to shelter me from the experiences that they went through and that they largely kept to themselves. Their arrival in Canada was a chance to reposition identity as British/Commonwealth immigrants to another part of the Commonwealth. It added another level of story, with the very explicit struggle for Civil Rights/equality happening just over the border in the States, and the less visible inequalities being lived in Canada (indigenous First Nations, French-English, Catholic-Protestant, Non-English-speaking immigrants, Commonwealth immigrants, Anti-Semitism, for a start).

Following my experience at the conference, I have begun to make a conscious effort to connect with others and myself, to own my mixed ethnicity in a way I never had before. Being 'Mixed' was to always be on the outside, not this, not that. My journey has led me to some wonderful people doing wonderful work and getting to be part of a meeting with 'my peers' was a great solace. It was a moment where I did not to have to prove or justify anything – display wisdom, insight or skill – it was enough to be present and acknowledge the fullness of who I am, and help however I can on the next part of this journey for all of us.

Figure 8.2 Rick with his dad

Figure 8.3 Rick with his dad

CHAPTER 9
Your career is a marathon, not a sprint

Ross Ashcroft

Figure 9.1 Ross Ashcroft

Figure 9.2 Ross and his children

I am in my local, with a pint and my iPad on the table, deciding how to start writing this chapter, on what promises to be a contemplative process of my journey into headship.

While I was pondering, I went to the toilet, where I met an older gentleman, who had been sitting opposite me. I gestured him through the door first. He thanked me and then we both set ourselves up at the urinal.

Then it happened.

'Alright mate, so where you from?'

This may seem like an innocent question. However, it is a question I've been asked a million times throughout my life. So, for the millionth time I answer, 'Just around the corner mate, although I was brought up in a small town called Halesowen in the West Midlands.'

I waited momentarily, until the inevitable follow up question came.

'No, I mean where are you actually from? Like where are your parents from?'

Now I knew what he was asking and I also knew my response would not suffice, as both my parents were born in England. Sometimes I try and give the most elaborate response, stating I'm a mix of 25 separate nationalities, naming each one, simply for my own amusement. However, on this occasion I did not have the energy, so I replied truthfully.

'Both my parents were born in Oldbury, also in the West Midlands – England.'

I could see this man's frustration. He looked over at me, which was disconcerting for two reasons. The first reason: I was still urinating and staring into another man's eyes is not a typical social expectation in the gents' toilets. The second reason: I knew he was trying to figure out a way to ask 'You don't look English mate, because you're not White, so what country are you from?'. I could tell him I'm the grandson of John Thomas

Ashcroft, a White navy veteran who served in World War 2 and operated a ship which transported Winston Churchill back to England. Instead, I zipped up my fly and went over to the sink to wash my hands.

The man took another tack and decided to tell me about Abdul, Syed and Mohammed, all of whom he works with.

'They are lovely blokes and you would really like them.'

I presume he is telling me this as he believes I am Asian and it's his way of showing me 'he has brown friends'.

Now, I could tell him about me, but in the simplest of terms, I'm a cliché. I'm a young man who experienced a coward physically abuse my mother, and seriously abuse me. I'm a young man who experienced school exclusions. I'm a young man who experienced homelessness on a number of occasions, including periods while at school, college and university. But, most importantly, for this book, I'm a young man who is dual-heritage/ mixed-race; I am a mixed Black Caribbean and White British educator.

This might seem like I'm portraying myself as a victim, but I assure you I have never seen myself as one. However, as I grow older, I realise the simple facts of the matter are that being a young man who is not White has had an impact on my life, which I would not have experienced if I was a young man who was White.

While it is a sad state of affairs, this became even more real to me when my first child was born. I was pleased she was born with White skin, blue eyes and blonde hair. I was happy, because she won't get asked 'Where are you from?', because everyone will assume 'she's one of us'.

However, the opposite occurred when my second child was born; with olive skin and much darker features, he is obviously a child with dual-heritage. Essentially, what I am saying is one of my children may have vastly different life experiences and interactions from my other child, simply due to the colour of their skin.

It is important to note at this stage, although I have had various difficulties in life, I have grown up to become a teacher, specialising in Special Educational Needs, whose career has progressed to a Head Teacher role. I'm not a black activist, and neither have I experienced much overtly racist behaviour towards me. Instead, it has been much more subtle.

I really noticed being treated differently in secondary school. For whatever reason, many teachers just did not have any real expectations of me succeeding in life. Granted, I wasn't the best behaved, but I achieved well academically. I remember being sent out of the room in Science for talking. Now, most pupils protest their innocence and this was no different, apart from the fact I was not actually talking. It was my friend from the row behind. He wanted to be sent out and even admitted aloud to the teacher that it was in fact him who was talking, and not me. The teacher was uninterested in his confession and sent me out anyway.

When I came back in, after 30 minutes, she berated me in front of the class. I explained calmly that it was not me talking and reminded her that the boy behind me confessed it was him.

'One day I'm going to be a teacher, and I will make sure no one I teach will be treated the way I'm being treated now,' I said.

'You will be lucky if you even get into college, never mind become a teacher,' she replied.

That struck me like a lightning bolt. Why would she say that? I was top set in English, Mathematics and Science. What would stop me becoming a teacher? As I said earlier, I don't see myself as a victim, so that lightning bolt charged me like nothing ever had done before. It stayed present in my mind through every challenge; it propelled me forward, determined to become a teacher.

Fast-forward several years later, more homelessness and rough sleeping persisted, but more academic achievements came along with it. I'm now on my Post Graduate Certification of Education (PGCE) course. Most teachers remember this as the dreaded training year. It is full-on. One of the hardest years of my life. I really struggled with the academic rigour of the course, especially the English skills test. Fortunately for me, I had an amazing tutor: Dot Heslop. She encouraged me to go for a dyslexia test, something I had refused for so many years. The test showed I was dyslexic, and what followed was academic support that was invaluable.

There were many things about this year which showed BAME education professionals were not in abundance. Out of my cohort of trainee teachers, there were two Asian guys and myself, at a university in a very multi-cultural area of the West Midlands. The same occurred on my teaching placements; I do not ever remember seeing another non-White teacher amongst the teaching staff, even though the schools were in multi-cultural Birmingham.

My first teaching placement was not successful in the slightest. Clearly, for whatever reason, I was not a good fit for the department. I was given Dance to teach and told to do what I know best, 'like street dance'. I have never taken part in, or taught, street dance. The same teacher was unhappy for me to teach any theory as she believed 'I wouldn't have that level of knowledge'.

Charlotte, another trainee from my course, was also placed at the school; she was seen as 'having that level of knowledge'. Charlotte was well versed in Dance and had also taken part in street dance for several years – interestingly, she was never asked to teach it. I was a dual-heritage male and she was a White female. I always found it interesting how differently we were treated throughout the placement. I am sure the teachers working within that physical education department would strongly deny any forms of racism, or discrimination exist. However, an obvious and clear bias existed between two trainees, with no real explanation to why.

Getting a teaching job in PE was now more difficult than ever. The government had cut funding for School Sport Coordinators (SSCO) and Competition Managers (CM), hence people in these roles were going back into teaching.

The market was now flooded with experienced PE teachers, resulting in my training cohort struggling to secure jobs. I applied to work with children with Special Educational Needs, which resulted in me being the second person in my trainee cohort to land a job. This made me incredibly proud. What followed was a whirlwind career where microaggressions and unconscious bias were rife.

In my first teaching position, in an inner-city Birmingham school, I was asked by my manager if I thought having cane rows in my hair was 'appropriate or professional'. These were professionally done, in straight lines and not patterned, and in my opinion very neat and tidy. I asked another member of staff who was also a teacher, with bright pink hair, a nose piercing and several visible tattoos, if management had ever asked her about professionalism. She laughed and replied that they hadn't, ever.

At the same school, I applied to become Head of Department. Several of the experienced teachers told me I wouldn't have a chance; I didn't understand why I wouldn't. I was an outstanding teacher, who had successfully improved the outcomes of my pupils. I got the job. One white member of staff said that the Black staff would be happy that one of their own is now in management. I was also asked several times to have difficult conversations with black colleagues outside my department as I was told that they would take it better from me.

I grew dreadlocks, again these were created professionally, to make sure I had a tidy image. I gained my first leadership role in a school in Shrewsbury, Shropshire. Compared to my previous county, I noticed just how much I stood out. Myself and the principal of the school were the only non-White school leaders in the county. I actually made the difficult decision to cut off my dread locks and have a 'normal' hairstyle to conform. I felt the need to blend in as much as possible.

It was at this time I went to my first leadership conference. Out of hundreds of professionals, myself, my principal and one other Black Head Teacher were the only non-White school leaders I could see. When we checked into the hotel, the receptionist was surprised I was there for the leadership conference and thought I had turned up for the wrong event. The other non-White Head Teacher I mentioned earlier was laughed at by a member of staff when she said she was a Head Teacher. She was then asked what she really did for a living. I was beginning to feel like I did not belong here.

Throughout my career, I have met people in senior positions who clearly have set views on race. I remember an executive Head Teacher in Walsall, who told me I was 'too aggressive' because I politely disagreed with him. He also told me that there was a reason that there aren't a lot of people like me in leadership positions. I asked him what he meant by 'people like me', but he didn't want to clarify.

Some people may read this chapter and say I was unfortunate or that these are isolated incidents. They may even argue that they aren't even incidents worth mentioning, as it is just me overthinking innocent interactions. I argue that unconscious bias, and the micro-aggressions that come with it, are widespread within education. If this was not the case, then this book would not be needed.

One clear example of unconscious bias is the number of times I have turned up to greet a visitor in reception in a suit and tie, and they presume I'm a Teaching Assistant. This has happened to me on numerous occasions, in numerous leadership positions, in numerous schools, in numerous local authorities. I do not know of any White leaders in education who have ever been mistaken for a Teaching Assistant, but do you know how many non-White leaders of education I know who have had the same experience? You've guessed it … numerous.

However, if you are reading this thinking there is no hope, you would be wrong. There is! I have recently secured my first headship at an amazing school, which I have always admired. They believe I have the skills and abilities to lead the school through the next stage of their journey.

The boy who was excluded from two schools, experienced homelessness, experienced domestic abuse as a child, told he would never get into college, never mind become a teacher, diagnosed with dyslexia and who experienced subtle racism throughout his career is now a Head Teacher at his very own school. It's been tough, really tough. But I got there. However, the exciting part is that this chapter is just one section of a very long story, and I cannot wait to find out what happens next.

But before I do that, I need to finish my pint. Watch this space …

CHAPTER 10
An epiphany

Ruhaina Alford-Rahim

Figure 10.1 Ruhaina Alford-Rahim

Last night, I had an epiphany. A realisation that came to me, I'm ashamed to say, for the first time in my life. An understanding of the meaning behind all those comments that I had thought were glibly made by my mother. Comments made to me as a child, growing up in suburban London in the 1980s and repeated to my children, now living in rural Devon.

I can reel off the comments. I can predict them before she says them.

'Don't let yourself tan; you will look too dark.'

'You don't look Asian; it's good people think you are European.'

'Because your husband's White and you've given your children English names, nobody will know what they are.'

This pride in being mistaken for a White person, fooling people into believing I am what I am not, the denial of my identity, never ceased to disappoint and hurt me, until now, until she shared with me what she did.

My mum, Yasmin Rahim, a bubbly, confident and incredibly capable woman, was born in Kenya and came to Britain in 1975 to marry my dad, Dr Sadiq Rahim. He had come to London, from Zanzibar, an island off the East coast of Africa, in the '60s to pursue his studies and undertake a Ph.D. in Physics. He was a brilliant man and although he passed away at 55, he achieved so much. As well as being a lecturer he had many businesses including a successful tutoring centre. He was a lay preacher at our local mosque and was the President of our Shia Muslim Community and used his position to develop community cohesion with other faith groups. He was always working, rarely sat down and slept very few hours a night. His ambition to be a Head Teacher was realised when he financed and set up his own school in Tanzania. This project was mostly about altruism, but I know that deep down he didn't feel he would ever become a Head in this country, despite his drive and ability. But he never really spoke about why.

Last night it all made sense to me. As we chatted over the phone, my mum mentioned that she had been listening to a Black Lives Matter discussion on the radio. She had been reminded of something that had happened back in 1976. She and my dad had put an offer on a house; she was pregnant with me and they wanted somewhere bigger. Since she worked for a bank, the mortgage had been arranged easily. All looked to be going well, when my dad called her to say that it was all off. The reason? 'They don't want to sell to 'Coloured' people.' According to the agent, the neighbours had pressurised them.

I felt sick to hear this, imagining the pain and degradation my parents must have felt. I had heard the stories of my dad's early days in London, where he and his cousin would attend church socials because people spoke to them out of Christian duty, whereas at other places they were ignored. I knew that when my mum first started to wear the *hijab*, the bank manager insisted she tied it behind her neck in a Hilda Ogden style. I remembered that it was only when Madonna made 'Henna tattoos' fashionable that I felt comfortable to put my hand up in school and expose my *Mehndi* because for years the girls in my class had asked why I had dirt on my hands. But none of this felt quite as blatant or as personal as to be rejected from a neighbourhood before even moving in.

We are a product of our experiences and if my mum's were of rejection because of the colour of her skin, then there is no wonder she seeks the sanctuary of light skin for her children. To be accepted and have all the opportunities that she perceives may be denied if it is immediately obvious that we are different.

I told her that I finally understood, and she explained that it wasn't just the experiences in this country, such as my dad being overlooked for promotion time and time again, or the looks or comments my mum gets after a terrorist incident. She had come from Kenya, which despite gaining independence from British Colonial rule in 1963, retained a hierarchy according to colour, with Asians sandwiched between White people at the top and Black people, very much at the bottom. In addition, India, from where her family originate, has a deeply embedded caste system that skews the way skin colour is viewed.

The desire to be the same is quite a powerful urge when you doubt your place in society or fear rejection because of your difference. For years I have judged my mum, cringed at her comments, feeling I am so much more enlightened than her. But am I really? I have never faced overt racism. Granted there were the *Mehndi* comments at my mono-cultural school where my best friend was a Black girl – the only other non-White child in the class. As time went on and London became more and more multi-cultural, I became a teacher and worked in diverse schools and felt accepted for who I was.

So why is it that I am so proud of my cut-glass English accent, that I would never wear a sari unless to an Asian wedding, that I anglicise my name to *Ruh Alford* and that I always feel the tiniest trepidation when I write my maiden name *Rahim* on a job application form?

If I am truly honest, somewhere deep inside, I anticipate rejection because of my race and religion. Whether it is my parents' experiences and behaviour rubbing off on me, or the noticeable shift in media coverage of Islamist terrorists, Trojan Horse incidents or anti-immigrant rhetoric on social media, I am not entirely sure.

I have now reached the point in my career that my dad dreamed of, I am the Executive Head Teacher of The Carey Federation in Devon. The schools are in rural villages in the heart of the countryside. All the children are White-British, so in some ways it feels like going back in time to my own mono-cultural school days, but there is one major difference. I am determined that the children in my schools have pride in their own agricultural heritage, coupled with a respect and understanding of all cultures, so they grow up to be global citizens. I feel privileged to be an educator and know that there will be no place in these children's hearts for racism.

As for me, I am working hard to be more open about who I am – starting with my name.

Figure 10.2 Ruhaina and her dad

An epiphany

Figure 10.3 Ruhaina and her mum

CHAPTER 11
Learning, growing and finding your light

Sabrina Edwards

Figure 11.1 Sabrina Edwards

Figure 11.2 Sabrina and her family

From an early age I always had a deep sense of justice, even if I wasn't yet able to articulate it. I remember watching 'Carry On' films, James Bond and the occasional Western as a child, laughing uncomfortably at the stereotypes they portrayed because everyone else was, but knowing deep down that they were offensive.

Both my parents immigrated here. My father from Grenada and my mum from Italy. They both had different experiences of being from a minority culture in England, which led to a confusing, and often damaging, set of views being imprinted onto my brother and me growing up. As a nine- or ten-year old child, I have a distinct memory of discussing my mixed heritage with my school friend, one of the only other mixed-race girls in my school at the time. We described ourselves as 'half-caste' (an acceptable term to some in the 1980s but a term I would never use now) but then proceeded to go even further back in our family histories to describe ourselves in terms of fractions! I thought my great-grandfather was Scottish, there was some Portuguese and Grenadian on my dad's side and that my mum was Italian. I think I decided on one-half Italian, one-sixteenth Scottish, one-sixteenth Portuguese and one-quarter Grenadian.

At the time I had no idea what this varied heritage actually meant or how it came to be so. I knew I felt uneasy with it, but I didn't know why. Around five years ago I was introduced to the 'Legacies of British slave-ownership' website and made the haunting discovery that I did indeed have some Scottish ancestry, in the form of a slave owner who owned a total of six descendants of enslaved Africans on the island of Grenada – my direct ancestors on my father's side. The story I had been told as a child about my Scottish ancestry was unlikely to be one of an interracial love affair but more likely to be as a result of rape. Finding this out so many years later definitely put a very different spin on that innocent conversation I had with my friend in the 80s.

I was 'exotified' throughout my childhood, especially during my yearly summers spent at the beach in Italy. People would stop their families to point and stare at us, and not always in ways that felt positive and welcoming. I was well aware of my differences. Questions such as 'Why does your hair get shorter when it's wet?' and 'Why doesn't it even look wet?' were innocent questions for the most part, but often there was a negative undertone that made clear that the way I looked (especially with the dark tan I would get by the end of six weeks in the sun) was undesirable.

Back in London, living in Tottenham, I was surrounded by diversity. Nevertheless, in many of the activities I took part in, such as dance lessons, I was one of the only children with darker skin. At the time, through media, books and magazines, we generally only saw people with pale skin and straight hair being lauded as beauty icons. I remember my 3rd year junior teacher, Mr Tharp, being the first and last teacher I ever had to teach us something positive about being Black. We learnt that Egypt is an African country; that the people of ancient Egypt were Black people, they ruled for thousands of years and created inventions that still cannot be explained. We learnt about hairstyles and we even had someone come in with hair dummies for us to try out some African hairstyles! He was a true inspiration and still is. The next time I learnt anything about Black people was in secondary school, where we started a history topic on the slave trade. What a disappointment that was. I recently found my old school exercise books and let's just say that the version of events we were taught was the epitome of a colonialist curriculum told only from one perspective. I remember feeling so sad at the time that the history of Black people started with slave trade; I knew this couldn't be true. If I had been a bit more courageous, I would have asked 'But what about what happened after the ancient Egyptian times and before the slave trade? Surely Black people were around doing something then, weren't they?'

After managing to get through the ordeal of secondary school (Tottenham in the early 90s was a brutal place) and the colourism that also existed within the Black community there, I left for 6th form college. I purposely chose a different area, so that I could meet new people. This was where I had my first experience with a teacher who, I felt, wanted to limit my expectations because of the colour of my skin. During an A-level psychology lesson, my tutor asked me where I was planning to go to university. I had my heart set on Exeter; they had the course I was looking for (a rare combination of Psychology and Italian) and it involved a move away from London, which both terrified and excited me in equal measure. When I told her my plans, she looked surprised.

'Hmmmm ... Are you sure you're going to ... you know ... *fit in there*?' she said.

For a split second I was confused and genuinely didn't understand what she could mean. And then the finer nuances of the conversation became clearer.

'Maybe you should think about going somewhere a little bit more ... you know ... where there are more ... you know ...' she continued.

She asked me whether I had thought about applying in London too and reminded me how hard it is to get into Exeter. I was crushed. She basically told me that not only would my skin colour be a barrier to being successful at a good university, but she also told me to lower my expectations of getting in somewhere like that and just stick to universities in London where I'd 'fit in'. What she didn't know about me was that I had become an expert in fitting in. I already had a wide range of friends from all walks of life and was beginning to perfect my skills in seamlessly drifting from one group of friends to another, whilst always being able to draw on my mixed heritage to make different groups feel at ease with me (more on this later). What did become clear to me was her view that no matter how much I thought I could navigate White society, I was still Black and should stick to places that had other Black people in it as I wouldn't be welcome anywhere else. Was she trying to protect me from racism? Maybe or maybe not. I'll never know her intentions. I do know that areas do not become diverse unless you make them so! I ignored her and put Exeter as my first choice anyway, although her remarks affected me and have stayed with me ever since.

Whilst clearing out the loft recently, I happened upon all the university essays I wrote for my undergraduate psychology degree. I came across two in particular: one on the need to decolonise the National Curriculum and the other on embedding anti-racism in education. Reading these essays reminded me of my original motivation for becoming a teacher. I wanted to be like Mr Tharp. To be that inspirational teacher that switches something on in a child; helps them to see who they are; where they've come from; and who they could become. I had such a wonderful vision for the educator I would be back then. Whilst reading those essays I wrote back in 1998 and 1999, I wondered where that person went. I have had many successful years of being a teacher and I hope I have been that memorable teacher for at least a few children along the way, but I have recently been reflecting on why it has taken for me to be a Head Teacher to fully realise that vision of being an active anti-racist in the workplace? Why was I not brave enough to challenge and transform the curriculum I taught previously, to ensure that the colonial outlook so deeply embedded in our education system was eradicated?

I worked it out. Conformity. I have had to dim my light in most of the schools I worked in; neutralise my Blackness so as to not make others feel threatened or intimidated; not rock the boat; not be accused of 'playing the race card'. I was afraid that by pointing out injustice, that I would be the one accused of racism. Now, this wasn't always because of overt policies or conversations where these things were made explicit, but in each school I worked in, something would happen that made it abundantly clear that many of my colleagues had extremely problematic views on people with darker skin tones, most likely based on the one-sided colonial education they had themselves received.

In one school staffroom, an experienced teacher asked me whether I could swim because she had heard that Black people have denser bones and just sink. I looked around for support from another member of staff who might step in and tell her that was extremely offensive, but it never happened. Nobody batted an eyelid. As a young teacher in my second year, I just didn't feel brave enough to speak up for myself and tell her how racist and offensive her comment was. In another school, well into my career when I had a good range of teaching and leadership experiences under my belt, I was told I should 'lower my expectations' when I announced to the Head Teacher that I would be applying for senior leadership positions. This was after being passed up for internal promotion twice and the position being given to someone in their second or third year of teaching each time. This was a school where if your face didn't fit, you weren't going anywhere near the Senior Leadership Team. When you looked at who was successful at gaining a senior leadership position and who was not, it was very clear what kind of faces did fit – and none of them were brown.

When I started my headship, after my first gruelling year, my school improvement advisor told me not to underestimate the impact of the fact that I was young, Black and a woman and that some people just wouldn't like it. I didn't want to admit that my skin colour, age or gender could have been the reasons why I had such a difficult time; after all, they hadn't prevented me from getting the job in the first place, had they? But I knew deep down that the staff, who took issue with me, had their own issues and I can't help but wonder if their reactions and behaviour towards me would have been different if it had been a white man making exactly the same decisions.

These are the kind of micro-aggressions we can't always put our finger on, but know they are there. From the parents who weren't expecting to see someone like me on the gates, because my name was 'Edwards', to the staff I overheard describing the upset reactions of some of our Black parents as them 'playing the race card' (rather than admitting there were many underlying racial issues going on at the school which had been brushed under the carpet for years); my first year was tough. But I made it through that difficult period. I'm now going into my fifth year of headship. I've recruited and trained a strong team. We've created an ethos of openness, honesty and continual learning. We are dealing with racism and sexism head on. I no longer feel like I have to make myself more palatable by not discussing my Blackness (even though I know that the lightness of my skin and the curl pattern of my hair has made me easier to accept in many of my previous roles), I feel like I am finally able to be that educator I aimed to be when I wrote those essays over 20 years ago. What saddens me is that even after 20 years, the issues I discussed in my essays haven't really changed at all.

My advice to you, if you are a new teacher just embarking on your career, with that vision for creating a better future for the next generation: be brave. We are now in a time where calling out racism in all its forms is welcomed and we need more brave leaders if we want to create the equal global society we've been dreaming about. People will make assumptions about you; some people may even try to limit your aspirations as they did for me, but as long as you don't limit your own aspirations for yourself, you will succeed. Don't let anyone dim your light; in fact, get yourself a brighter bulb!

CHAPTER 12
Children can't be what they can't see
Breaking the cycle

Sarah Hobson

Figure 12.1 Sarah Hobson

Figure 12.2 Sarah, her dad, and her sister Sasha

DOI: 10.4324/9781003498612-13

Since I can remember, I had always aspired to become a teacher. As a child I took no resistance and taught my soft toys how to spell. My dad, who taught English as a second language, was a huge inspiration to me and my next steps were inevitably going to follow in his. I saw how he was fulfilled by teaching and helping others and I wanted to do the same.

I did go through a stage where I wanted to become an actor, and spent lots of my childhood in stage productions and attending castings; I managed to become a member of the National Youth Theatre and got a place working in New York with an affiliated American Youth company, BAYFEST (British American Youth Festival Theatre). These early experiences helped me to decide what I wanted to work towards. Working in the Arts at a young age taught me that I definitely did not want to become an actor, but that I absolutely loved the Arts and the experiences they had provided me. They had positively shaped my early years and the passion I developed in understanding scripts, production and most importantly reading people and character, was what I wanted to pursue. I wanted other young people to feel the same way I did about Drama.

At school, I never saw any teachers that looked like me. I never saw any leaders that looked like me and even my dad, who was White, didn't look like me. Despite this, my aspirations remained the same and I decided I wanted to teach Drama. However, being a brown girl in an urban London school, performing, dancing, singing and learning an instrument were not the 'in thing' to be doing and actually a lot of the Black children frowned upon a positive work ethic. This then became a larger issue, as I was trying hard to study and a particular group of Black girls took offence to this. I became their target and they made my life a misery. Despite these horrible experiences, I strived to do well at my GCSEs and came out with reasonable grades, enough to get me to my next stepping-stone to undertake A Levels.

It was odd. I never thought of doing anything else. I never even contemplated an alternative. I didn't ever think I wouldn't go to university; my route was already laid out and

I did exactly what I planned. I went on to university and studied Film and Theatre, I then went on to do my PGCE in teaching Drama at The Central School of Speech and Drama and had a surprising setback. One of my tutors asked to meet with me regarding one of my essays and said they had noticed that my written work read like I was struggling. I was sent for some testing at the dyslexia centre in London, which came back with a report that I had problems with my processing. In fact, my comprehension was in the 97th percentile of the country, whereas my working memory fell into the 7th percentile. The report stated that they hadn't understood how I had managed this far.

The truth is I hadn't managed. I had worked bloody extra hard, blood, sweat and tears, to get my GSCEs, A levels, degree and then my PGCE and had always wondered why it felt so hard. Was it because I was brought up in a single-parent household with my dad and my sister? Was it because I went to a rough high school? Was it assumed that I would be less able and my needs had been ignored?

My first placement during my PGCE training was in a north Watford school. I was a born and bred Londoner and had never been further up the M1 than Harrow. Watford was a new experience and the biggest shock I had was the socio-economic makeup of the pupils. I had never been around so many White British children and it took me time to adapt. Halfway through my placement, I remember one of the sixth formers saying to me that I should go and have a joint with them. When I retorted that the suggestion was highly inappropriate, the child said that because I was brown then, of course, I smoked weed. Something hit me that day. I was being stereotyped as the 'cool, brown, Drama teacher' and I hated it, but had no idea how to break down these stereotypes.

I managed to secure my first official teaching job in the April of my training year. I had struck gold, landing myself a Head of Drama position at a private school. Now, bearing in mind that I had never really seen a private school, let alone worked in one, I didn't know what to expect. I was the youngest member of staff by at least ten years and the only brown teacher.

There were two brown students and within months I noticed they gravitated towards me and took Drama GCSE. Last summer, I attended the wedding of one of them and her mother mentioned me in her speech as a woman who provided her daughter with a positive role model.

I didn't stay long at the school. I felt morally wrong and thought my skills would be better suited in a state school, not to mention I felt like I wanted to give something back to the state. I moved on to another local secondary school, which was larger, busier, more forward-thinking and dynamic. I loved it there and felt I fitted in right away.

A few years down the line and after having my second child, I started to think about career development. I was becoming bored of being a Drama teacher and wanted some more responsibility. I was an aspiring Assistant Head Teacher, yet whenever I mentioned that this was my plan, I was laughed at – literally. I had formed a reputation as a strong and outstanding classroom teacher, yet was never seen as anything other than that. Despite working on whole school projects and joining the Continuing Professional Development team to raise my visibility, no one saw me as more than just a Drama teacher. I began to wonder what it would take to be recognised as a potential leader, but also why it hadn't happened already. Did I not fit the image of a leader? After all, I hadn't seen any brown leaders in any of the schools I had worked in or gone to.

During this period, I was doing some Drama teaching outreach at a local Pupil Referral Unit and through this route I heard of an assistant headship at another referral unit. I thought, this is my chance, I had nothing to lose, went for the job … and got it.

Much to the surprise of my current school, I had managed to make the leap to leadership. The role took me totally out of the classroom and was a baptism of fire. However, all my training and skills in analysing character and behaviour really came into their own with the children there. Understanding behaviour and trauma became an area of expertise for me. I felt like

I had done a degree in mental health and behaviour before I left. As part of this role I was expected to visit many stakeholder schools and liaise with Head Teachers and Senior Leadership Teams across a large number of establishments. I noticed that when I arrived in these schools, there was often an assumption that I was a support worker, admin worker or teaching assistant (who are all hugely important roles, but are not leadership positions). I began to recognise the facial expression that I received once I had introduced myself as the Assistant Head Teacher. It was always one of surprise, or readjustment, which I liked to pretend I hadn't noticed. However, three years down the line and the same reactions became a trend, and although I never wanted it to be the case, I began to admit to myself that it was my appearance that was evoking these reactions. I also found it very shocking that on so many occasions, I would be the only person of colour in a room. Moving into a very different forum of leaders as a new senior leader was eye opening and it slowly dawned on me that I was a rarity in this body of leaders in education.

I eventually got to the stage where I missed the classroom and mainstream school, so sought to find a new role in mainstream education again. I took a position which was a sideways move into a state school.

I began my journey at my current school, teaching English and seconded onto the Senior Leadership team, covering aspects of two members who were on maternity leave. This encompassed some Special Educational Needs Coordinator and Inclusion work, which was an area of special interest and expertise for me. Despite me being the only brown person in the room, yet again, I felt that the consistency of being in one place would allow the time for staff and students to recognise my role and to dispel that notion of surprise as to what I did.

Working with a new and fresh Senior Leadership Team empowered me to demonstrate what I thought I was capable of achieving and within the year I had secured an Assistant Head position on the team. The staff body was young and committed to delivering high standards, which dovetailed nicely with my leadership ethos. I was informed of a potential deputy headship position at the school, which covered Inclusion and Behaviour, and although I had never striven to be a Deputy, I felt it was natural for me to work towards the position. After all, I had been an Assistant Head for nearly six years.

I was very aware that the current Head and other deputies had been White males and I did feel a sense of threat that maybe I was too different to meet the needs of the role. Despite being highly professional, I always had at the back of my mind that I was a good 'code switcher' and could apply myself to different situations effectively (maybe it was my Drama training). I had my nose pierced and had tattoos. Sometimes my hair was big and sometimes braided. I was aware that in a role such as this, I would need to be myself and that might not be what they are looking for. I was brave enough to present like this in my interview, after all what you see is what you get, and if they wanted to appoint me for who I was, then great!

I have been a Deputy Head Teacher for nearly a term and have found the role challenging and rewarding, but interestingly I have found it such an achievement on a personal level.

At no stage growing up did I see deputies who looked like me. At no point in my career did anyone say to me you look like a senior leader. I may not fit the stereotype or box of what a senior leader looks like, however, I do a damn good job and am a well-respected member of the team. My focus is on the children that I work with and providing them with a quality education, but I also realise that I am changing children's mindsets, as they are also learning that leaders can also look like me.

CHAPTER 13
Overcoming stereotypes
Embracing your value on the path to leadership

Symone Campbell

Figure 13.1 Symone Campbell

Figure 13.2 Symone – mini me

DOI: 10.4324/9781003498612-14

We had moved from a community that was one of the most ethnically diverse districts in London to a predominately White area when I experienced my first encounter of racism. I was a young Black seven-year-old child having to put up with chanting of the 'N' word from White children in the neighbourhood and bullying at school in the playground on a daily basis. When another Black family moved into the neighbourhood, the same children would shout, 'Oh look, you have someone to play with now.'

At first, I did not quite understand why these children were so hostile towards me and at first I chose to ignore it, that was until the bullying got physical. I regularly reported the bullying to the midday assistants supervising in the playground, but unfortunately there was never any action taken. As a result, I chose to take matters into my own hands and began to fight back. This became a regular occurrence in the playground for weeks until I was reported to my Class Teacher and was removed from the playground into detention for a week. There were no consequences for the bullies who stirred up this anger within me and I felt deeply frustrated by this injustice.

After a few weeks I decided to break the silence to my mother, who arranged a meeting with my Class Teacher to find out why the school had not done anything to address the bullying and to highlight that the anger and fighting was totally out of character for me. Once the Class Teacher had discovered that the root cause was bullying, he was apologetic and reassured my mother that he would investigate the bullying. Fortunately for me, he did take action and the bullying stopped immediately. It was only then, that I began to thrive at my new school.

My parents could not reiterate enough that 'Once you have your education and knowledge, no one can take that away from you.' Other reminders were: 'Unfortunately, when you are Black my dear you have to work harder than others, because no one is going to hand you an opportunity on a plate.'

When I started in my first (non-educational) managerial position as a young, naive 21-year-old, initially my leadership was met with resistance. I rapidly discovered that when people think of leadership – a young Black woman is not the first picture that springs to mind. After a while I became accustomed to the fact that I wasn't what people expected, but I used this as fuel to motivate me, which made me more determined to progress. Although I found it difficult not to take it personally, I would remind myself of the phrase 'positive mental attitude' which was my manager's favourite saying.

Although there were no people of colour who were senior managers in the whole organisation, I was fortunate enough to experience the power of mentorship from three senior managers at different stages of my career, which I found to be effective in helping me to achieve my potential at work.

Despite these positive experiences, I still had to battle with prejudices. The typical micro-aggressions – the assumption that every Black employee has to be the junior member of staff; to be less qualified despite my credentials; questions about work ethic or performance; passion which may be misinterpreted as aggression; and occasionally feeling misunderstood. Colleagues with whom I had established working relationships over the telephone, but when we eventually met in person, would look shocked to discover they had been speaking to a young Black woman. The first occasion I was quite offended, but then I learnt to enjoy exceeding people's expectations of me.

I recall one day, arriving at work wearing my natural hair and a colleague stretched out her arm and attempted to touch my hair, but I recoiled with disgust, feeling shocked and angry that an attempt was made to stroke my hair like a pet. I thought to myself, why would you want to stroke my hair? When I wore my hair straightened there was never an interest to stroke it then. In hindsight, if this incident were to happen again, I would educate my colleague on why this would be considered as inappropriate.

I would experience unconscious bias comments such as 'You would like this top' and I would question 'Why is that?' and my colleague responded, 'Because it is African'.

Although some of these examples or comments may have been unintentionally offensive, the key point is we all have biases and although unintentional one should reflect about how the recipient perceives the offence. It is very similar to challenging the perception that children have of bullying. There is a stereotype of what racism is, but unfortunately if you do not understand the different degrees or levels of racism, it may not be recognised as racism.

As a result of some other negative experiences I faced, it led me to begin doubting my leadership skills and competence. When applying for new roles, I even went to the extent of removing my photo from my LinkedIn profile and not ticking the ethnicity boxes on the data collection sections of the application forms, so that recruiters would not identify my ethnicity until I arrived at the interview.

Years later, I still found myself constantly having to prove my value as a Black leader, despite working in various sectors, experiencing extra scrutiny in every role. The ability to direct, lead and motivate are essential to any leadership position and establishing the credibility to do so still comes with many challenges. The experience was always similar in every workplace and every conference I attended – I would immediately notice that there was no one else in the room who looked like me. I began to feel like a 'lone ranger', having to create my own support structures and feeling as though I needed to censor how much I told colleagues about myself or my personal life.

After the murder of George Floyd, which sparked protests, it triggered some very strong emotions within me. At first, I felt liberated. Finally, I felt people were beginning to listen. However, that emotion quickly turned to a combination of anger, deep sadness, anxiety and confusion. It is very sad that it has taken the killing and long periods of unrest and protesting against the multiple Black Americans killed by the police – Breonna Taylor, Ahmaud Arbery and many others – for our voices to be heard. To add to this trauma, as well as being in the middle of an unprecedented pandemic, I was now having to hear about people who were unable to process the information they received about racism – responding in a dismissive, defensive or detracting manner. I found this period to be both mentally and emotionally draining and exhausting. Just because it is not your experience, or you are not aware of it, it doesn't mean it isn't real.

The subsequent Monday following the protests, I remember having to contemplate how I was going to respond to colleagues if they asked me, 'How was your weekend?' or 'How are you doing?' Unfortunately, I did not feel comfortable or confident enough to be vocal about how I was truly feeling, and this left me with a sense of guilt that I chose to opt out of addressing the situation.

I was pleased to see that many organisations were posting bold statements on their social media feeds about how they were in support of change, yet I suspect 'true change' is yet to be seen.

Now we have the opportunity to be role models, not only for pupils, but also to help shape more positive experiences of new colleagues entering the organisation, in order to thrive in their positions. Building a diverse and supportive culture is much broader than having discussions in a meeting or publishing an equality statement. Diversity in and out of the classroom will continue to grow, so it's essential we prepare pupils to adapt to an evolving world and embrace those different from themselves.

It is imperative to have diverse leaders and governors in school leadership, running our schools to improve the awareness of different races, cultures, religions and economic status, ensuring they understand and can identify with the experiences of their whole school community and, more importantly, having open and honest discussions.

There is a need for more accountability, for people to be advocates for change, to improve and develop systems to improve the way diversity, inclusion and equality is managed, and working towards eradicating systematic racism in the workplace. School improvement and strategic planning, reviewing recruitment processes – including having diverse interview panels, talent pipelines, training and ethnicity pay reporting and other actions such as having the intention to work with a more diverse range of suppliers – all form part of the way forward.

On reflection now, as a Black School Business Leader, my personal and professional experiences, both good and bad, have helped to increase my awareness of how my behaviours can affect my work environment: leading by example; being mindful of the language I use; the tone I set with my own team; and challenging inappropriate behaviour. Undoubtedly, we all have some self-reflection to undertake, on things we can do better and ways we can positively contribute to change. I am committing myself to being a part of the solution; if you have the same desire, I urge you – now is the time to act.

CHAPTER 14
Focused, determined and resilient

Yvonne Davis

Figure 14.1 Yvonne Davis

My ambition, from the age of seven years old, was to be a teacher. I was the first in my family to attend university and at an early age, I realised that there were low expectations of Black children. I personally experienced challenges as a child and as a Black teacher. I now have a career that has spanned for over 40 years, teaching in different local authorities and in a range of schools. Since the 1970s I have networked, collaborated, led and managed in a range of settings. I have succeeded with the support of my family, by being self-motivated, determined when times were difficult, resilient and always with the aim of making a difference.

In the backdrop of inflammatory rhetoric led by Enoch Powell and his infamous 'Rivers of Blood speech' I started my first teaching practice. Here, I experienced first-hand the hostile atmosphere of a school environment. During a normal school assembly, I sat with eyes peering at me and with derogatory name-calling as I walked into the classroom. Returning to my student accommodation, I was upset, anxious and distressed; I phoned my mother. My mother was supportive and encouraging and her words were always reassuring, she said, 'That is why you need to be there!'. That was all the inspiration I needed and other than that, I knew she was right!

Part of my first lesson was to teach the school community about a Black Briton who was born in England and I used myself as an example. I am a Black British-born woman with a Caribbean heritage, as both my parents were born in Jamaica. They were welcomed by the government into this country, as members of the Windrush generation. During my time at school, I had already experienced the name-calling, the monkey jumps and the 'put-me-downs' by teachers who pigeon-holed me for the new Certificate of Secondary Education exams and stereotyped careers. A career in teaching was far from the minds of my teachers. What did not help was that I was born and lived in Wolverhampton, where the inflammatory rhetoric led by Enoch Powell was rife and influential.

Throughout my career I have wanted to make a difference. As a Black woman, both directly and indirectly, I have celebrated diversity, strived to improve young people's lives and worked to enhance educational provision for all children. I have had an incredible career, in which I have led from the front, inspired, trained and guided teachers to improve the quality of learning.

I started my career in 1978 as a class teacher in Coventry, where I was one of only two Black teachers in the county. My post extended beyond daily teaching to meet the needs of the BAME communities in schools across the city. I wrote stories, and produced a booklet of the resources that teachers could use in class, which was published by the Minority Ethnic

Group Support Service, a branch of the Local Education Authority. My mission was to celebrate diversity, through the stories we had at that time and share as widely as possible with the local schools. However, it soon came to light that the service appointed teachers at a higher grade, which became noticeable to others who recognised the work I was doing. There was no other option but to address this with those at the top in my school, who then offered me a higher grade with embarrassment.

Headhunted by Birmingham local authority, I was appointed to teach in the Handsworth and Lozells area of the city – culturally rich, but economically deprived. During my time in Handsworth (1985–1995), I applied for three posts and was successfully appointed, which broadened my experience moving up the career path. I had an incredible time in Birmingham, not only working in schools but with the community, who embraced my support for their child and my role as a listener for their needs. There was a vibrant community who spoke out about discrimination, which was experienced on a daily basis through the systems in place.

My final post in Birmingham was as Deputy Head Teacher and acting Head Teacher (1996–2000). During this time, I applied, and successfully became, an Associate Adviser while still Deputy. The focus was on working collegiately with Early Years providers to improve the quality of provision in the maintained and the private sector, community day nurseries and the local playgroups. Being given the opportunity to work with a wide range of providers had a profound effect on me. It gave me a deeper understanding of how children learn and how one nurtures their development. I soon learned that working collaboratively is a key factor in raising achievement, which is crucial for the future of our children.

Working in isolation can be limiting to the progress of any school, which should be enriched by focused minds, expertise and discussions. With this belief, I have worked closely with other schools both primary and secondary, for the benefit of staff training, joint senior leadership meetings and school self-evaluation.

In 1996, I represented the voice of Deputy Heads on the Strategic Community Team of leading educator Sir Tim Brighouse, Birmingham's Chief Education Officer. The team comprised of local authority members and community groups in the city. The ground-breaking collaboration focused on the underachievement of Black boys and White working-class boys.

The leadership skills of Sir Tim Brighouse had a lasting effect on me, showing the importance of connection with your 'customer'. This was a man who was passionate about improving the futures of the children. While sitting in his board-room with community representatives, and local authority officers discussing the underachievement of Black Caribbean boys in the city, he was held to account by outspoken community leaders who wanted answers there and then. I was extremely impressed by his ability to keep the meeting focused, accept the anger and acknowledge what the local authority were failing to do.

I have made it my duty to observe and celebrate the work of teachers in school. It is right to say, apart from a child's parent or carer, teachers are the next powerful influencer in their life. Sir Tim Brighouse listened to teachers in his busy life as Chief Education Officer. He often arrived unannounced at schools and spoke to the teachers about valuing our work. I received three treasured handwritten letters from him that are still in my possession, congratulating me on my work. A 'thank you' to the school community goes a long way: listening to ideas; giving responsibility with support; providing an environment where all members of the school community are valued.

In 2000, I relocated to Hertfordshire to take up the post of Head Teacher at a primary school in Watford, becoming the first Black Head Teacher in Hertfordshire. I had a successful headship, recognised by the local community who nominated me for Woman of the Year in education in 2003 and 2005. I attended the Guildhall in London in 2005 with more than 400 women selected for their achievement and contribution to society.

In 2004, I was appointed Primary School Adviser in Buckinghamshire to work with 26 schools in support of their vision. I was leading learning, monitoring provision and training governors. At this time, I trained as an Ofsted Inspector and retrained when I returned to headship in 2008. My wider remit was to work with the Early Years team to improve the quality of provision under the umbrella of school improvement. I successfully engaged with Early Years leaders and Head Teachers by initiating practitioner training, a conference, and an opportunity to visit Reggio in Northern Italy. After learning together, I organised the sharing of good practice across the county where interested participants opened their doors for practitioners to view the outcome of their training.

In 2008, I returned to Hertfordshire in a Head Teacher post, rising to the challenge of amalgamating two failing schools. I had to work extremely hard, not least because there was a strong community resistance to the local authority's decision to the merger. The parent community were challenging as I stood outside welcoming everyone each morning; the response was torture as they stared blankly. I remember being asked by a member of the local authority, who stood with me one day, how long I was going to stand out and welcome them. My reply was until they welcome me back. Within a matter of weeks of taking up the headship of the school we were alerted to a notification of an Ofsted inspection. The school received a notice to improve. However, the report praised my strong leadership, giving a clear sense of direction and in 2009 my leadership was graded as 'outstanding'.

I am proud of the initiatives I have introduced: our Forest School; opening a nurture class; and a new eco-building to expand our therapeutic environment for school and community use. I am proud of leading in a school where professional learning has created leaders for the future, where staff feel valued, supported and embrace learning to learn. Therefore, with this ethos, we have a happy school. We evaluate together and share ideas, and we're open and honest without feeling threatened.

Let's step back in time. During the seventies and eighties, the teaching journey was riddled with overt racism for teachers and children, with policies and practice which categorised you and stilted individual progression. Until the introduction of the Race Relations Act, it was a difficult working environment. There was no support when you saw or heard inappropriate language and actions. I once reported an incident, when I had been asked to teach in a disadvantaged area where the parents refused to have a Black health visitor work in the school, and excuses were made. I experienced micro-aggressions from staff and children. However, I did not give up developing enough confidence to professionally challenge the negative attitudes and damaging actions experienced by ethnic minorities. I have reflected on the experiences in which racism presents itself in different ways, some are intentional, some are based on ignorance and misunderstanding, because the curriculum is Eurocentric. I have taught in a variety of schools in urban and rural settings, mainly White British and they can be at different stages in addressing this issue. The leaders of the school have a significant role to engage with their school community, including parents, to change attitudes and deliver continuing professional development for their teachers, when they review and implement an inclusive curriculum for all children.

I therefore return to my mother's words to me as a student, 'make a difference', and it is through my practice that I feel I have succeeded in that. In Dame Jocelyn Barrow's words, 'Each One Teach One', this is what I have used to lead and is a prime factor in education, in that the school community all have a significant role in learning from each other. Learning to learn for the future of our children.

Dame Barrow DBE, a qualified teacher, arrived in England from Trinidad in 1959 to teach. She was shocked by the level of discrimination she witnessed and experienced against Caribbean and Asian immigrants. This inspired her to set up the organisation, Each One Teach One, to help families to navigate the education system. Racial discrimination and racism were dominant in all areas of life. We still have racism, which is systemic in the policies and practice in all professions. There has been improvement, but unfortunately we have a long way to go, as the progress has been too slow.

Teaching is a rewarding profession, as the children bring joy in seeing them make progress, when they share their learning and make even the smallest steps. Today, anyone going into the profession must remember: You are not alone. At times, it can feel like it is a lonely job, but the support is there from experienced mentors and leaders.

My focus, throughout my career, was to lead by example; model expectations, share my experience in a learned way, giving staff the space and the trust to share their feelings without judgement. I have not let my colour pave my destiny, as painful as it may have been at times. I have embraced the challenges which have driven me. There is an inner force at work, as one can espouse all the leadership skills, but it is in the delivery and the belief you have in your vision, shared and accepted by everyone in the school community, that will go a long way in leading a successful school.

CHAPTER 15
Culture and ethos
Additional chapter

Diana Ohene-Darko

> *The views and examples shared in this chapter are those of an individual serving school leader, rather than being official NAHT policy or advice.*

If you are reading this, then you have spent time with 13 of the most courageous people I know. Pouring your story out in written form is not easy. It takes courage and a leap of faith; opening yourself up to possible scrutiny, disbelief or even backlash. Thankfully, none of those have been true for the book you are reading. Instead, this book has already provided countless professionals with a source of inspiration; a source of strength and determination to succeed in a profession that has so much to offer; a source of solidarity. In these pages you will have found compassion for each other and for you.

When considering culture and ethos, it can be thought of a little like, what came first, the chicken or the egg? In order to establish the culture and ethos of a school, it starts with you. Trying to become a school focused on equality and equity of outcomes takes planning and preparation, self-reflection as well as living out common values every day. In considering this, most schools have between three and nine core values. Values by which the organisation advertises their identity as part of a unique selling point, in addition to holding others to account by these values, living these values and making these values part of the very web of that organisation; a golden thread running through the most intricate tapestry.

So where to begin? Becoming an anti-racist and gender-equal place of education, indeed a school equal across protected characteristics, requires a long-term, strategic plan. The first year should be spent in raising awareness and helping staff to understand the journey you are on and the reasons for this. That first year is a year of awakening to the issues and how best to address them for your school, college or institution. Staff in the first instance, need the opportunity to self-assess their own beliefs and values. Personal reflection is vital to understanding not only yourself but also in helping to understand others. By truly acknowledging where we sit on a racial bias continuum, for example, we can set out the work needed. A lot of reading and research is required to understand wider issues of racism and bias and the impact on individuals and communities. The writers of this book have shared their lived experiences in the hope that these instigate change for the better. The next year can be spent thinking more about engagement – with staff, with pupils and the wider community. Which groups do you need to engage with more? How will you do this? What does engagement look like across all stakeholders and members with protected characteristics? This could take the form of parent ambassadors to help initiate and sustain communication between the school and harder to reach groups, for example. It might also consist of an annual cycle of events and information sessions, workshops and continuing professional development. Another year or years beyond that would be about embedding your vision as part of the overarching culture and ethos of your school – this is who we are, this is what we stand for and this is what we do.

Whilst we wait on (national) change directed from the government, we can start the work ourselves. Leaders, according to their school values, must strategically plan change. Working backwards can help begin the process. What is the change you want to see? If all stakeholders are fully equal and there is equity of outcomes, what will staff, pupils and your wider community be thinking, feeling, saying and doing? Of course, there are already books out there to support the creation and growth of culture and ethos within schools. This section offers a lens on racial equality and social justice in building a more equitable culture and ethos within places of education. What follows are some practical steps in how to create a more equitable culture and ethos. Some will be quick wins, whilst others will require longer, more sustained work with specific intentions in mind.

Structural systems are sometimes often difficult to unpick when thinking about where to start. This can be both overwhelming and off-putting. Instead, think about *people*. People are the greatest resource and of the greatest value. Start here.

The first *people* to consider are the leaders. Leadership teams must commit to the work. Create safe spaces in order to have open discussions, making the uncomfortable comfortable. Without opening up to vulnerability, change will not happen. Being vulnerable means that there is a non-judgemental approach to wanting change; a reflective means to creating safe boundaries that will ultimately hold other *people* to account, whilst maintaining the dignity of another person and always, always acting with integrity. This a call to courage, a call to be brave, a call to do the right thing because it is the right thing to do. Everybody needs to have a voice, none louder than another – make space at the table because 'I' am coming to sit down.

Set equality as an agenda item for senior leader meetings. Have members of staff come and feedback on their areas of responsibility. Check actions arising/met at least every other week. Without gaining valuable input from all stakeholders, the *people*, a clear path cannot be planned for going forwards. Start small and grow. Ask staff to take part in a steering group/ an action-focused group that is rooted in the organisation's values and mission statement so that all outcomes are intentional. Start with the questions outlined above. Where do you want to be in a year, two years, five? What impact do you want you see? Set ground rules for the discussions and keep to them. Ensure that there is both psychological safety for those within the group and confidentiality, unless there is a safeguarding issue. Let them be the lead communications team, driving improvement from the ground up. These discussions could be hooked around a central (big) question such as, 'Why aren't we talking about race?' or 'What impact does racism/ adultification bias have in our school?'

In assuming that racism or biases exist, leaders can be better prepared in the approach for change. The same is true of Ofsted's report into sexual harassment in schools – you have to assume it happens at *your* school. What, then, is the policy on dealing with racism and biases, for example? Does your school specifically outline racism, the different biases and how they might show up in interactions? Or is it a case of having umbrella equality objectives, lifted from the Equality Act 2010? Is there a clear equalities policy? Equalities objectives, far from being umbrellas could be specific, working targets, adjusted year on year, with a view to a three-year, long-term plan (see above). By all means have overarching objectives, then break these down into specific actions with timeframes and the person(s) responsible. Hold staff to account for their duties and responsibilities where equality is concerned. Make this part of appraisals and school improvement more widely.

On a lighter note, start a staff library for issues of equality. Share recommended reads and have a bank of non-negotiables (even if it is extracts) for leaders and all staff. Root your school improvement in sound pedagogy and research. Create a routine of bite-size information drops through sharing of vlogs, blogs and extracts (in addition to the recommended reads). Audit your school library for authors from different backgrounds (including race, gender and sexual orientation). Are your *pupils* reading a range of authors? Do they have access to books that represent them? The same is true for texts, images and resources used in class – are these representative of your pupil and staff population? Can they 'see' themselves in the curriculum? Can your website be translated into different languages, not least the languages of the community, the *people*, you serve? Think about putting equality on your cycle of (weekly) staff emails and continuing professional development.

There has to be bespoke and ongoing continuing professional development (CPD). By engaging with the subject matter, as with any initiative, staff must seek to understand the issues at play and their impact. Since this is not just an initiative, more a way of being. It will not be the case that everything will be right for everyone all of the time; rather, they hope to get most things right, most of the time, for most people – everyone learning together; everyone learning everywhere. CPD has to be carefully thought out in order that there is clear communication and learning about key issues. Although unconscious bias training can be viewed negatively with little impact following this, there are successful ways in which this can be approached in order to shift mindsets and behaviours. The trick is not to aim for one hundred per cent, fully-fledged change or a 180-degree turnaround in attitudes. The greater success is found in changing one thing by even 1% consistently and regularly. For example, if you wanted to change the (negative) interactions with pupils at risk of exclusion, it could be that there is a whole school, staff effort to speaking in an even tone, not raising voices and being respectful. This as opposed to forming judgements in the moment, not hearing a pupil out or demanding respect over showing it. The one per cent change is in doing something differently, and more positively, than you did before. If it happens again, just say to yourself, you will do better next time. Hold yourself to account for that change.

The same is true for the *parent community*. What biases come into play when interacting with them? Do you hold specific biases when it comes to engaging with an outspoken parent versus a quiet and unassuming parent, for example? What about when engaging with parents from different backgrounds? There are socio-economic biases in play, age and gender biases, race and culture biases. I wonder what thoughts run through your mind about a parent based on what you assume to be true/have judged about them. To give a wider example, I have an affinity bias for the elderly. I automatically relate to them because my father was an 'older Dad'. I was always protective of him, seeing him as more vulnerable because he was older (age-bias?). I assume the elderly are vulnerable and need my help. Actually, many of them are entirely self-sufficient and fiercely independent, just like my late father was!

By exploring racism and bias in all its ugly truth, we are saying: I am here. I have shown up. I want things to change. I am committed to growth. In the same way that there have been educational drives to learning about adverse childhood experiences and addressing this through a trauma-informed approach, there needs to be a drive to understanding racism and its impact on individual victims as well as whole communities. Four years on from the brutal murder of George Floyd and with subsequent high profile racist incidents such as the strip search of Child Q, it is not enough to say that lessons need to be learned. It is now time for action. A time for examining our societal conscience, putting structures and systems under a microscope, and asking, 'Is this good enough?'

As humans, we each have our stories. Fourteen are contained in this book. Each one holds a message of hope and (a quiet?) determination. Although race has been made for the structural advantage of some, it is a biological result of two people who came together and yet is a powerful force for identity and belonging.

Culture and ethos come down to one overriding value: compassion. Can you meet me where I am, for who I am? What common ground do we share that allows us to live in harmony under a banner of values that we each hold dear?

ADDITIONAL READING

Recommendations from the Stephen Lawrence enquiry
Recommendations from the Sewell report
Recommendations from the Practice Report on Child Q
Dare to Lead, Brene Brown (YouTube)
Do Better, Rachel Ricketts
Black and British, David Olusoga (children's version also available)
Why I'm No Longer Talking to White People About Race, Reni Eddo-Lodge
I Belong Here, Anita Sethi

Resources

Useful anti-racism toolkits/audits can be found either on, 'The Key' (for school leaders) or DiverseEd as a form of self-assessment prior to planning change.
Lyfta – human stories

CHAPTER 16
Curriculum change
Additional chapter

Danielle Lewis-Egonu

> *The views and examples shared in this chapter are those of an individual serving school leader, rather than being official NAHT policy or advice.*

> Organic farmers are not focused on the plant; they are focused on the soil. This should translate to education.
> (Sir Ken Robinson)

There is a constant discussion in education around the evolution and content of the curriculum, and there should be.

I think of a school as an organic entity, with inclusion representing the heart and curriculum representing the brain. Both are vital, necessary for survival and growth and have equal importance in creating an environment where all children can succeed.

There are many ongoing conflicts in education relating to the dominant paths that should lead the way.

We are constantly striving for the balance between the deep routed English process of embedding high-stakes accountability into the institution of education, which comes with Ofsted, standardised testing, GCSEs, league tables and so on, and teaching knowledge and skills, which prepare young people for the world and to become global citizens.

Fundamentally, there is an awareness that we need to teach children to pass exams, but we also need to teach them how to learn to engage with the world and its people.

It is a reality that curriculums evolve and reflect changing factors such as social influence and educational leadership at its moment in history. However, the essential focus of educators in state schools is to offer and preserve democracy and equality and seek to change it if it's not there.

If schools reduce and marginalise the teaching of knowledge, it will only increase the undemocratic and unequal features of our society. Children deserve to have access to knowledge of the things external to them and related to their circumstances. If we only teach pupils using the knowledge they bring to the classroom or pick up through experience, we will only succeed in continuing to reproduce educational inequalities.

Simply put, the curriculum in our schools needs to be reflective of the cultures, races, ethnicities, genders and social classes found in Britain (alongside other marginalised communities) and be academically rigorous and rich.

If we want pupils to develop the skills of analysis and evaluation, they need to know things, and we need to help them acquire the knowledge to develop these skills.

Across our curriculums, we need to allow children and young people to look at:

- **Issues**: These help children and young people get the knowledge and identify the problem.
- **Actions**: Guide children in contemplating and deciding the activities to take or analyse the ones taken.
- **Change**: With a deep level of knowledge and understanding, you and they can evoke change, whether that be in a maths problem or the environment around them.

Knowledge gives you language.

Language allows you to articulate thoughts and gives individuals power.

Power and language give you access to opportunities.

If we truly seek to understand who we are, where we come from and where we are going, then we must explore and recognise OUR history in a nuanced fashion and allow children this opportunity as well.

As schools 're-design' the curriculum, are they imposing their lack of knowledge and understanding onto children? Or are they setting a high bar for all children's educational experiences and educating themselves?

We need to think about what is left out of the curriculum and who.

Providers of curriculum resources can support teachers and schools in building their subject knowledge and awareness of facts relating to the questions posed above. The aim of fact-learning is not to learn just one fact – it is to know several hundred, which form a schema that helps people understand the world. Schools need support with this from teaching resource providers and the government.

Since May 2020, when many began to have a heightened awareness of the impact of racial discrimination, not just on life chances, but on one's very existence, the world refocused and took a deep breath, but we are in danger of allowing this momentum of reform and self-analysis to stop. One question we have asked for decades is an example of this halting of momentum. Why are Black Caribbean and Free School Meal eligible white boys still the most underachieving group in education? We have been working on a Victorian model of education, which is abstract to today's needs, for far too long. Frankly, doing the same things repeatedly and expecting a different outcome is madness in a world that has changed significantly since this era.

By diversifying the curriculum, we are upskilling our workforce, addressing bias, enhancing pupils' emotional wellbeing, securing access to high-quality provision, and encouraging peer support among young people.

This truly has to be the way forward for education.

ADDITIONAL READING

Stacey, C. (2018). *A Life Sentence for Young People: A Report into the Impact of Criminal Records Acquired in Childhood and Early Adulthood*. Maidstone: Unlock. Retrieved from www.unlock.org.uk/wp-content/uploads/youth-criminal-records-report-2018.pdf

CHAPTER 17
Recruitment and retention of a diverse workforce
Additional chapter

Lorna Legg

The views and examples shared in this chapter are those of an individual serving school leader, rather than being official NAHT policy or advice.

THE DUTY

The recruitment and retention of a diverse workforce is not simply a laudable aim, or a moral imperative; it is a legal duty. As set out in the overview to The Equality Act, 2010, it 'legally protects people from discrimination in the workplace and in wider society'.

Alongside this overarching protection, The Act also asserts two additional policies which support equality, and which are relevant to educational establishments:

- Positive action – recruitment and promotion
- Public Sector Equality Duty

Positive Action

Positive action allows for under-represented groups who share a protected characteristic, for example sex, race, or disability, to be given preferential treatment in order level the playing field. Positive action is permitted under the law in limited circumstances as set below.

- There is evidence that a particular group is under-represented or otherwise disadvantaged in the workforce.
- The employer does not have a policy of treating persons who share the protected characteristic more favourably in connection with recruitment or promotion than persons who do not share it.
- The appointment process has objectively assessed the merits, skills, abilities, and qualifications of each of the candidates.
- The individual is as qualified as the other candidate to be recruited or promoted.
- The action that you are taking is a proportionate way of addressing any under-representation or tackling disadvantage.

The Public Sector Equality Duty

The Public Sector Equality Duty, which applies to all public bodies, such as schools and colleges, compels consideration of all the individuals their work affects. This includes employees and, in schools, the pupils and families served, making the governors responsible for ensuring, through the policies and services they provide, that they:

- Eliminate discrimination, harassment, victimisation and other conduct that is prohibited under The Equality Act 2010.
- Advance equality of opportunity between persons who share a relevant protected characteristic and persons who do not share it.
- Foster good relations between different people when carrying out their activities.

To ensure transparency, and to assist in the performance of this duty, The Equality Act 2010 (Specific Duties) Regulations 2011 require public authorities to publish:

- Equality objectives, at least every four years; and
- Information to demonstrate their compliance with Public Sector Equality Duty.

To ensure compliance with this Act, public sector organisations are required to collect and provide 'proportionate and relevant' statistics on diversity, in order to show progress and set equality objectives.

Therefore, it is clear that discrimination must be acknowledged, addressed and corrected, wherever it is evident, and that organisations are enabled and encouraged to do so.

THE PROBLEM

So, 14 years later, how effective has this legislation been in reducing inequality and ensuring equality of recruitment and retention of a diverse and representative workforce? In 2024, discrimination remains evident in the ongoing disparity between the diversity of our society and the representation of the leadership of our schools, colleges and other organisations.

Paul Whiteman, General Secretary of the NAHT, commenting on Equality Pay Gap Day 2022, stated that leaders from a Black, Asian or minority ethnic background risk facing a 'double hit' in relation to pay as a result of inequalities in the pay system. These are legion.

From a 2020 study by UCL's Institute of Education, it was found that 46% of all schools in England employed no Black, Asian and minority ethnic teachers. In addition, Black, Asian and minority ethnic teachers were found to be under-represented in senior leadership roles (UCL Faculty of Education and Society, accessed 14.12.20). The same is true even in ethnically diverse areas, where there can sometimes be a greater percentage of staff of more diverse heritage.

In the government's evidence to the School Teachers' Review Body (STRB), 2022, it is evident that teachers of Black and Asian origins are more likely to progress into leadership roles than their White colleagues, which looks encouraging, but not when they are, by the same measure, less likely to progress into headship. How is it that ethnically diverse teachers of experience and undoubtable ability (as evidenced by their promotion to leadership roles) are still finding it harder to progress into headship? Morally, this cannot be justified.

According to the government's own statistics from February 2021 (accessed online 27.4.22), 92.7% of Head Teachers are White British. Looking deeper, out of the remaining 7.3%, only 1% of Head Teachers are Black, with 0.6 % of Head Teachers being from Mixed White and Black African or Caribbean heritage. Head Teachers of Asian origins make up 2.2% of this group (not including Heads of Chinese origin, who number 0.1%), with Head Teachers of mixed Asian backgrounds constituting 0.3% ('Other' and 'Unknown' account for the remaining 3.1%). As a simple comparison, in 2011 (last census) 19.5% of the general UK population did not identify as White.

This lack of representation is not only a legal and moral issue, it is also detrimental to better leadership of schools, and ultimately has a negative impact on children's outcomes. Diversity is a strength; it makes for better decisions; better policy; better outcomes; it means role models for individuals with diverse characteristics and for diverse communities; it means better opportunities for Black or ethnic minority people; it encourages creativity in problem solving, through taking account of a range perspectives; it means diverse experiences and opinions are accounted for in planning and practice; it prevents stagnation and concentration of power in a small elite, avoiding 'baked-in' structural inequality, instead promoting opportunity.

Matthew Syed, in his best-selling book on the power of diverse thinking, *Rebel Ideas*, provides lots of examples and research where representative demographic diversity improves the performance of organisations:

> an increase in racial diversity of just one standard derivation increased productivity by more than 25 per cent ... In any domain that requires an understanding of broad groups of people, demographic diversity is likely to prove vital.
>
> (p. 66)

THE IMPACT

So, the data tell us we have an issue, but what does this look like and how does it feel? Here are a few anecdotal experiences linked to recruitment, shared within hours of me asking for examples from the NAHT Leaders for Race Equality Network in February 2022:

> Went for a job in a London Borough. At the end when it was my turn to ask questions, I asked whether the governing body was diverse. The response was 'we are rich and white!' I didn't get that job.
> (Christine, Head Teacher)

> I went for a job as a Head Teacher. Went for a walk around and spoke to the chair of governors. All seemed to go well. I was asked for a detailed personal statement which I did. I then got an email back saying they had changed the process to ensure that there was no bias and that I would be asked a series of professional questions instead. I answered all of them to a very high standard but didn't get shortlisted. When I asked why I was told there was a disparity between who they met and my answers ... Basically it seems I was more intelligent than they thought. A process that was set up to eliminate bias actually ended up disqualifying a Black candidate.
> (Frankie, 10.4.22)

> An acquaintance working as an Assistant Head Teacher (AHT) went for the substantive Deputy Head Teacher (DHT). On the first occasion was shortlisted, interviewed and a non-BAME applicant chosen. 6 months later new DHT also left. AHT becomes acting DHT. Job is advertised again, and she applies. This time round nobody is shortlisted. She remains acting DHT. Third time job is advertised, is shortlisted, successful at interview BUT then offered the job on a rolling monthly basis to see if she can do the job (same job she's been doing as acting DHT for

months). Chair and Head met with her to offer it as a temporary position to be reviewed monthly. Job was advertised as a substantive post but when it got to her turn became temporary and on a monthly basis...No wonder we are overly stressed or leave the profession in droves.
(Christine, 10.4.22)

I went on an interview last year for Head Teacher at a local school, was up against the Deputy Head Teacher and another candidate, both white females and the panel of all white governors. Later that evening I was told that the governing body had decided not to appoint and that I would get feedback. A week later I was told that I was the strongest candidate and that I smashed all the tasks, but in the interviews my answers were 3.5s with some 4s and that the governors wanted someone who scored all 4s, so the deputy would be acting head and that the job will be re-advertised! I found out two weeks ago that the acting head was made substantive, no advert was published on school website or anywhere!
(Poonam, 10.4.22)

These examples show how the reality and perception of inequality persists, contributing to lack of representation, and a sense of unfairness and stigma, which can prevent people of Black, Asian, or minority ethnic backgrounds from even applying.

As the UCL report stated in its key findings:

> Racism and associated inequalities are at the forefront in BAME teachers' minds in conversations about retention, not workload.

> The racial literacy of all school leaders and their commitment to equity and social justice are important for creating a supportive organisational culture.

While the recruitment and retention process can appear to be transparent, without an understanding of bias, stereotyping and prejudice, the long-listing, short-listing and interview process itself is flawed: it relies upon first impressions – good or bad – which can be misleading and fatal for diversity, where cognitive bias, stereotyping and prejudice are at play.

THE SOLUTIONS

In reading this, as an employer, you are already on the path to greater equality. As a teacher or leader of diverse heritage, you can use this information (including the resources listed below) to empower you to take action against unequal treatment and dispel any stigma you may feel in even raising these issues. What matters is to understand the strength there is in diversity and to share the duty we all have under The Equality Act; share the problems those with protected characteristics face and share the simple solutions all organisations can enact:

1) Accept that lack of diversity in education is a problem – that diversity is a strength – and commit to finding solutions. Help others to realise their legal and moral duty to encourage diversity and support equality.
2) Understand the issue in your own school: How many governors, leaders, staff and pupils have a protected characteristic? How do you know? What are the outcomes of pupils with these characteristics? Why?
3) Address the issue: plan for equality; ensure all policy considers your Equality duty; ensure all staff and governors are aware of the protected characteristics and their collective duty under The Equality Act; consider positive action where appropriate.
4) Ensure training on bias and aspects of equality in education are part of your annual INSET, termly Staff Meeting plans and training for governors, at least annually, as for safeguarding.
5) Where you are lucky enough to be of diverse heritage, or have people of diversity in your school community, seek views, representation and engagement in your school's equality and inclusion plan, perhaps in a lead, advisory or mentoring role (although be sensitive to any workload or personal barriers to feeling singled out due to ethnicity or other protected characteristics).

Governors retain overall responsibility for recruitment. This may still be mediated by a local authority (LA) representative, who could guide the governing body and remind them of the legal requirements in terms of transparency and equality. Beyond LA control, a MAT can choose to be guided instead by a recruitment agency or in-house HR department. This calls for extra vigilance and scrutiny around adherence to all equality aspects of the recruitment process. It is clear from Ofsted's statement in the Education Inspection Framework that this is not a duty any governing body can afford to ignore:

Inspectors will assess the extent to which the provider complies with the relevant legal duties as set out in the Human Rights Act 1998.

However, the countless equality statements all organisations write, in compliance with the 2010 equality law, run counter to the proof in practice: look at the facts and faces before you. Training is essential, in particular for the governing body, but also for staff. Crucially, there remains a lack of understanding in some schools (governors, leaders, staff, pupils and families) about the psychology of bias, stereotyping, prejudice and discrimination which work together to perpetuate inequality.

Unconscious, or implicit bias training can make a real difference to how we see each other. Cognitive bias comes in a myriad of forms: take confirmation bias, which makes us cling to information that supports our existing beliefs, rather than seek out evidence to the contrary; or in-group bias, where we are more likely to favour members of our own social group; or fundamental attribution bias, which makes us attribute other people's behaviour to our existing stereotypes, while disregarding or excusing our own, similar behaviours. Bias creates shortcuts in our thinking that lead to prejudice, unfairness in recruitment, and discrimination if we do not educate ourselves and challenge our own thinking.

The other side of prejudice is stigma; many with protected characteristics do not achieve to their potential, due to a toxic combination of victimisation, and diminished self-confidence leading to a self-fulfilling prophecy. It can take years to overcome the negative self-image that such prejudice creates, if ever. If we have any care at all for our children's futures, how can we stand by and allow such waste of potential?

Seven years after The Equality Act, The Lammy Review (2017) set out to look at outcomes for people of Black, Asian and Minority Ethnic backgrounds in the Criminal Justice system. It found that 'Despite making up just 14% of the population, BAME men and women make up 25% of prisoners, while over 40% of young people in custody are from BAME backgrounds.'

It is clear that this disparity of treatment remains as testament to discrimination. Those who end up in the Criminal Justice system will have faced inequality from their earliest years, potentially from birth and throughout the education system, due to structural and societal factors we are all responsible for. One of the aims of the Review was: 'A justice system that works better for those who are BAME and poor will work better for those who are White British and poor too.'

This principle also works for schools. Any organisation that places equality (equity) at its heart will improve outcomes for all those suffering from inequality of opportunity. This is why diversity in leadership – especially leadership in education – plays such a vital role (alongside other public services) in promoting equality, so that all our children are able to thrive and contribute throughout society.

I will leave the last words to Matthew Syed:

> The success of organisations, as well as of societies, depends on harnessing our differences in pursuit of our vital interests. When we do this well – with enlightened leadership, design, policy and scientific insight – the pay-offs can be vast.
>
> (p. 245)

ADDITIONAL READING

The Anna Freud Centre has created a series of Podcasts (accessed online February 2022) www.naht.org.uk/Our-Priorities/Our-policy-areas/Equality-diversity-and-inclusion/ArtMID/824/ArticleID/1499/Talking-racism-and-mental-health-in-schools-podcasts-from-the-Anna-Freud-Centre

Twelve examples of Cognitive Bias – Contributor: Neil deGrasse Tyson, n.d. www.masterclass.com/articles/how-to-identify-cognitive-bias#12-examples-of-cognitive-bias

The Equality Act, 2010 (which replaces the Sex, Race and Disability Discrimination Acts and incorporates Age Discrimination) (Accessed online April 24 2022) www.gov.uk/guidance/equality-act-2010-guidssance

Ethnicity Pay Gap Day – Comments by Paul Whiteman, NAHT. n.d. (January 8 2022) www.naht.org.uk/Our-Priorities/Our-policy-areas/Equality-diversity-and-inclusion/ArtMID/824/ArticleID/1457/NAHT-Comments-on-Ethnicity-Pay-Gap-Day-2022

Government Evidence to the STRB, 2022 (Accessed online April 24 2022) https://assets.publishing.service.gov.uk/government/uploads/system/uploads/attachment_data/file/1060707/Government_evidence_to_the_STRB_2022.pdf

The Lammy Review, 2017 (Accessed online April 24 2022) https://assets.publishing.service.gov.uk/government/uploads/system/uploads/attachment_data/file/643001/lammy-review-final-report.pdf

Positive action in promotion and recruitment, n.d. https://assets.publishing.service.gov.uk/government/uploads/system/uploads/attachment_data/file/85014/positive-action-recruitment.pdf; https://assets.publishing.service.gov.uk/government/uploads/system/uploads/attachment_data/file/85015/positive-action-practical-guide.pdf

Matthew Syed, 2019 *Rebel Ideas – The Power of Diverse Thinking* (Publisher John Murray)

Antonina Tereshchenko, Martin Mills, Alice Bradbury, n.d. *Recruitment and Retention of BAME Teachers in England – Report from Institute of Education (IOE) at University College London (UCL)*. https://discovery.ucl.ac.uk/id/eprint/10117331/1/IOE_Report_BAME_Teachers.pdf

School Teacher Workforce – Statistics form the Government – Published February 18 2021 www.ethnicity-facts-figures.service.gov.uk/workforce-and-business/workforce-diversity/school-teacher-workforce/latest

Printed in the United States
by Baker & Taylor Publisher Services